My Gift of Now

My Gift of Now

A Collection of Short Memoirs

Elynne Chaplik-Aleskow

PUSHCART PRIZE-NOMINATED AUTHOR

MILL CITY PRESS • MINNEAPOLIS, MN

Mill City Press, Inc.
322 First Avenue N, 5th floor
Minneapolis, MN 55401
612.455.2293
www.millcitypublishing.com

ISBN-13: 978-1-63413-453-8
LCCN: 2015906635

Book Design by B. Cook
Author Photo by Susan Chaplik

Printed in the United States of America

Contents

Introduction

I am a blessed woman. Even with the tragedies you will read about my life, I have been blessed. The beloved family members I lost in two plane crashes existed and left beautiful, inspiring and timeless legacies. Meeting the love of my life and marrying for the first time in my early forties fulfilled my search for my best friend. I am the eldest of four loving sisters born to parents who are exceptional humans. Building careers that fascinate and motivate me continues. I was founding General Manager of a PBS affiliate making me Chicago's first female television GM; I am Distinguished Professor Emeritus of Wright College; I am a Pushcart Prize-nominated author published in over thirty anthologies including Chicken Soup for the Soul and This I Believe. Memoir is a natural fit. I have true stories to tell and to share. Some will make you sad and others will make you laugh. I hope my stories inspire. This nonfiction story collection was requested by my readers. The anthologies in which my work is published have been wonderful sources for the exposure of my writing. My thanks and deep appreciation to the many anthology publishers and editors who continue to publish my stories in their books. It has been through their publications that readers have read my work resulting in the request for a collection of my memoirs and essays.

My past, present and future converge in ***My Gift of Now***.

ECA

Dedication

This collection of memoirs is dedicated to individuals whom I cherish: my beloved husband Richard who is my everything; my precious mother and father; my three wonderful sisters and brother-in-law; my loving family; my loyal friends; my delightful students; my devoted readers; and my gracious colleagues. A special and enduring thank you to those readers who have shared their feedback with me. Their belief in my writing has touched me to my core. Of my many favorite comments from readers is this one: "*You are dynamite wrapped in silk!*"

One

Twice in One Family

MORE THAN LIFE

Pushcart Prize Nominee

When my mother was a girl, she went to a fortune teller during a night out with friends. The fortune teller told her that she would experience a life event of catastrophic proportion midlife.

"Who believes in fortune tellers anyway?" she thought.

And yet, it happened. My mother has known the ultimate happiness and has lived the ultimate tragedy.

When I would have sleepover parties during my grammar school and high school years, I would find my friends gathered around the kitchen table late at night listening to my mother telling her stories about her life. Every girl would sit there mesmerized by her voice and her animation. She was a housewife actress, a born oral historian. Even today, my teenage girlfriends who are now sixty-five years old quote from my mother's stories which they heard over fifty years ago.

My sisters and I planned and hosted an eightieth birthday party for my mother. We compiled many family members' wisdoms and quotes that she had passed on to us through her stories over the years and put them into a book which was distributed to every guest. We had family and friends come to the microphone and read a quote or thought from the book after introducing themselves and stating their relationship to my mother.

As she watched and listened, my mother had a faraway look. She was with us, listening and enjoying this tribute to her. Yet the full tapestry of her life had holes that could not be filled by toasts and testimonials.

As she listened to the words and stories that she had learned from her parents, family and friends and that she had passed on over the span of her life, her private focus turned to February 12, 1963 when she lost her mother, my beloved grandmother, in a plane crash. Through her strength and her faith, she continued her life and inspired a legacy of family through which my sisters and I built our lives. One of the greatest legacies my grandmother left us was showing how to love. She passed this natural gift on to my mother.

One of my treasures is a picture I have of my grandma in her housedress. My mother's image of her mother is different. She has told me that she remembers her mother always stunningly dressed. Whenever my grandmother would come to school, my mother has said that everyone would turn their heads admiringly toward her mother. That always made my mother feel so proud.

She suddenly thought of the fortune teller and the prophetic words that would come to pass. Eleven years after my mother lost her mother, on December 20, 1974, she lost my father and my youngest sister Ivy in another plane crash. My mother had just turned fifty.

My mother and father had been married thirty years when they were brutally and untimely torn apart. My father was fifty-five. My parents gave birth to four daughters. Ivy died at sixteen. She was the family gift.

My mother started to cry. She felt their presence as she sat listening to family members reading quotes from her birthday celebration book.

When we finished the program, we all took our seats. It was now my mother's turn to go to the lectern and take the microphone. This was her moment.

As she began to speak, I looked at her face. My mother and I are twenty years apart. I could remember most of her birthdays. With each year I watched her beauty mature. Physically she was a truly stunning woman but it was her ability to empathize and persevere that inspired awe. I thought of my mother's words about the pride she felt as she looked at her own mother. At that moment I understood. My mother's face glowed. Reflected in her eyes were the loved ones of her present and her past.

I remembered a trip my mother and I had taken to New Orleans when I was single. It was very special to me because it was just she and I. We walked blocks together enjoying the city's unique sights and atmosphere. Every street had signs inviting us to come in to storefronts for a fortune reading. New Orleans' seduction was irresistible. We opened a door and entered. A man asked me to follow him into a room for a Tarot cards reading and my mother accompanied a woman to her reading area.

The fortune teller asked me if I was married. I answered "no." He then looked at my cards and announced to me that I would never marry. After a few more inane predictions, we were finished.

I returned to the front of the store and sat down to wait for my mother. I waited and waited. I kept looking at my watch and wondering what her fortune teller was telling her. Finally my mother emerged from her reading. We left the shop and began walking down the street hand in hand.

"You tell me first," she said. "What did the fortune teller tell you?"

"He told me I would never marry," I calmly replied.

My mother stopped and looked at me. Her eldest daughter who was single and involved in building a career had just been told the curse of all curses.

"Oh please," she answered in disgust. "He did not know what he was talking about."

"What took you so long?" I asked. "What did she tell you?"

"Well," my mother began, "she asked me if I was a widow. I told her I was and she told me that she was too. Then she told me her life story."

This time it was I who stopped and looked at my mother. "What?" I asked in disbelief. "She told you her life story?"

"She needed an ear," my mother answered softly.

"Did you pay her?" I asked incredulously.

"Of course," my mother answered.

Growing up, wherever I went, I would be stopped by strangers and asked if I was Miriam Chaplik's daughter. Nothing made me prouder than to look in the mirror and see a face looking very much like my mother's looking back at me. Some of our similarities and many of our differences made for a devoted but tumultuous relationship. We could be warriors with wills that reflected a mother's and her first born's struggles. It was not easy for either of us. Yet deep within the foundation of our beings, there was a bond that was stronger than our disagreements and differences.

My mother had taught me to be a human being before I focused on gender. That made me fearless and free to be an independent and self-sufficient woman.

My mother had been a stay at home mom. However, she encouraged her daughters to become professionals. As I look back on my life, I realize that it had never been part of my awareness or identity that being female could be an obstacle to doing and achieving anything I wanted to accomplish. My sisters would say the same thing.

My mother has faced the devastation of her life with an uncanny grace and strength. There is no bitterness in her. She does not curse fate. She focuses on the blessings she has in her life, not the deficits. A great part of this ability to survive unimaginable agony and loss is her faith and her belief in family.

The catastrophe the fortune teller predicted happened twice in my mother's life but she survived, allowing love to guide her way. Her life is an example of how to live through tragedy and to love through devastation with courage and dignity. It is my good fortune to have been born to this woman to whom I owe more than life.

THE RED PEN

My thoughts turn to what has been with me for weeks. I am thinking about a past boyfriend whom I met again by chance. I cannot get him out of my mind.

He was not my boyfriend. He was the very special friend of my beloved sister Ivy when she was in high school. Ivy was sixteen when she died in a plane crash with my father.

Ivy was sister number four, the baby, although in many ways she was probably the most mature within her short life. She was a very rare young woman who had the ability to empathize like few people I have ever known. She was stunning physically and within. She had long wavy brown hair, oval chocolate brown eyes and a smile that mesmerized. Her gentleness and insight were the foundation of her poise that was well beyond her age.

Seeing her friend David again was an overwhelming experience. I could only think of Ivy's description of how she first met him while walking down the hall of her high school. She had told me that she knew instantly that she had to find out who he was. It was a romantic and womanly moment in her life.

I look at the face of this incredibly handsome man who is now in his late thirties. He is still single. I hug him and he returns the warmth and greets me by the nickname Ivy called me. My heart aches in response and yet I am filled with an indescribable fulfillment. I am looking into the eyes of someone who shared so much of my sister's life in a way that belonged only to them. I am thankful that she had whatever they shared. She would sometimes ride on the back of his motorcycle, her long dark hair waiving in the wind. I am thinking how glad I am that she rode on a motorcycle. I am grateful for every moment and experience she enjoyed in her life.

I tell him that I am so happy that they shared a special relationship. He shakes his head and smiles sweetly and shyly. He is a quiet man with an intensity that he also had as a boy. It was only to Ivy that he would open his heart. She would often listen to him for hours and advise him. She never told anyone what they talked about but I know she reached him in a way no one ever had. He needed her and she was there for him as she always was when you needed her.

After the accident David came to our home and sat in Ivy's room shaking. He looked at my mother, my sisters and me but he could not speak. His silence eloquently expressed the depth of his loss.

I often wondered how he was able to express his grief. I wrote about mine. My ability to express my feelings through my writing saved me after the accident.

For David it was in his smile and private memories that she lived on. They shared the same birthday. I would always love him for being part of her life.

In time David chose his moment to express his grief in a college English class. He was not sure that he wanted to go on to school, but he decided to try it and enrolled in a community college.

His teacher assigned a composition about 'the most important memory or experience of your life'. For whatever reasons, David was ready to talk for the first time about the loss of his beloved friend. He opened his soul and poured his heart into his paper.

When David received back his composition, it was filled with red ink marks. Spelling and grammar corrections were everywhere. There was not one comment about his subject. There was not one word about his feelings. There was not one phrase expressing condolence for his horrific loss. David dropped out of college. He became a successful businessman.

It would be years later after our chance meeting that I would hear about David again. I was utterly shattered by the words I was hearing.

In his early forties David learned he had cancer. His doctors had missed the diagnosis at first. He was in a wheelchair and his father had brought him home to die. Home was the house where he was raised, the house in which he and Ivy had spent time together as a teenage couple.

I knew what I had to do. It took everything in me to do it. I pulled up in front of his house. His father had a wheelchair ramp constructed off the garage. Two full time nurses shared shifts.

My heart was beating so fast and hard that it hurt. I knocked on the door and the nurse opened it. There he was. David was sitting in his chair. He raised his head as though it was a weight and his eyes met mine. That shy sweet smile was still there and as ill as he was, he was still that stunning young man.

He was very weak and I had to put my ear close to his mouth so I could hear him.

"I talk to her every day," he whispered.

I tried with all my strength to contain my poise. I did not want to chance embarrassing him in any way. My eyes, however, filled with tears.

"She is with you, David," I answered smiling back at him. "She is with you."

Then we sat together my hand on his and I read him the story I had written about them.

I think of Ivy's favorite song, *Color My World* by the group Chicago. The melody is beautiful, the lyrics loving and embracing. Like her life, like their love, the song is unusually brief yet hauntingly unforgettable.

HER FIRST GRANDCHILD

She is one of the great loves of my life. I lost her in a plane crash February 12th, 1963. The memory of my maternal grandmother Fannie Lebedow inspires me every day of my life.

I was my grandma's first grandchild. The bond between us was magical. One of my greatest treats as a little girl was sleeping over at her apartment. The room I slept in had twin beds. They were very high and fluffy. I always needed help getting in at night.

One morning my grandma came in to check on me and I was not in bed. The window next to the bed was half way open. Her apartment was on the third floor. She panicked thinking that I might have fallen out the window until she realized that I fell out of bed and in my sleep rolled under the bed. Years later we always shared a good laugh about that morning's discovery.

My grandmother was a tall woman with striking silver hair. She was handsome and stately in her carriage with a soft smooth skin that always smelled like fresh Palmolive soap. People would turn their heads toward her when she entered a room.

She was my grandma, a woman whose love for me was unconditional and giving. Loving her was natural and easy because she loved me back with such genuine joy and caring. It always felt good to be around her. I looked forward to seeing her, touching her and smelling her scent. With her I shared many of the happiest moments of my childhood.

One of the greatest legacies my grandmother left me was showing me how to love. She passed this natural gift on to my mother as well.

One of my treasures is a picture I have of grandma in her housedress. My mother tells me that she remembers her mother always stunningly dressed. That is not the childhood memory of her that I cherish, however. In her housedress she would take me grocery shopping and would tell me to pick out any candy I wanted. I always got the pretzel stick. I would hold her hand as we walked doing errands, returning home in time for the delicious lunch she would prepare for me. Her kitchen pantry filled with desserts was like Disneyland to me.

As I grew older, my grandmother became a friend with whom I could share my feelings. One day my mother and I had the worst argument we had ever had. I was twelve years old. I packed my belongings, willed my precious board games to my sister Linda and ran away from home. Of course the place I ran to was my grandmother's new apartment that was fortunately a few miles from my home.

When I arrived, she fed me and waited until I was ready to talk. My grandmother never pressured me or forced me. Our relating was easy and empathic. Her legacy of listening without judging is one I have tried to implement in my relationships.

A few years after losing my grandfather, my family convinced my grandmother to take a vacation in Florida. She was with my mother and youngest sister Ivy at the beginning of her holiday. Before they left for home, my mother found a small hotel for seniors and my grandmother stayed on for twelve more days.

My beloved grandmother never made it home. The commercial plane she was on hit a squall during the first ten minutes it was in the air and crashed in the Florida Everglades. Everyone on board was killed. My grandmother was sixty-seven.

I can touch the raw agony of that day when we found out that we lost her like it was yesterday. I was seventeen and about to graduate from high school and head to college in the fall.

We were assured her death was quick but I will never really know if she had time to be afraid. That question tortures me when I allow myself to think about it.

In losing Grandma Lebedow I lost one of the great loves and friends of my life. I hope she would be proud of the woman I have become. I smile at her picture every day. Frozen in time in her housedress, she smiles back at me.

GOLDEN HANDS

Golden hands was the way we spoke of my grandfather Isidor Chaplik. One of his sons, my father, Rubin Chaplik, inherited his gift. Both my father and grandfather were meticulous craftsmen. My dad invented and patented the first automatic coffee maker for restaurants. Until my grandfather's retirement, my father worked alongside his father in a family factory that my grandfather built from scratch when he came to this country as a teen from Russia. All my uncles were part of the business but it was my father who shared his father's talents. My grandfather and my father could build almost anything.

When my parents decided it was time for our family to move from an apartment to a home, my father designed our house and oversaw every detail of its construction. He even included a soda fountain which my mother eventually begged him to empty of its goodies because my sisters and I spent so much time tasting and devouring.

One day while shopping, my mother saw a chandelier which she loved and wanted to hang in our home. When she learned the price, she quietly shook her head and, almost in shock, left the store. That night she told my dad about her find and its price. About three months later, my mother drove to pick my father up at the factory. Dad motioned to her to come inside. He asked her to follow him into his work room. There, hanging in all its beauty and glory, was the fixture my mother had wanted.

"Did you buy it?" my mother asked.

"No," my father answered. "I made it."

Stunned, my mother smiled at my father while alternately staring up at her gift.

"Golden hands," she said. "Thank you."

My sisters and I grew up with the realization that we lived with a man who could fix anything. A woman can get spoiled easily with that good fortune. My dad would bring home all kinds of toys, my favorite being a model train. The problem was that we could never get close enough to play with these toys because my dad was playing with everything. There was one exception. I recently realized that although I am right handed, I can only play left handed pool because my father, who was a lefty, taught me how to play on the billiards table he bought.

My dad was a Renaissance man, a human being who loved life with a passion and joy that were awe inspiring. He was the father of four daughters and watching him master his varied interests was a lesson my sisters and I enjoyed learning. From photography to flying his own plane, his joie de vivre was a gift he shared with not only his family, but with all who knew him.

My father believed in himself and his talents. That example of determination, focus and commitment was a life legacy he gave to us. He was our protector and mentor. He was a creative inspiration in all he did.

From his father, my dad learned many lessons: love of family; a work ethic that was solid and uniquely successful; pride in being Chaplik; generosity to others in need. My mother, sisters and I were grateful for this special man in our lives and the honor of sharing his genius. My dad's warm charismatic smile and his larger than life energy touched many.

My father joked that he took to the skies because he lived with five women. We always laughed at that joke and were happy to see him enjoy his true life's passion.

My father was also blessed with a beautiful singing voice. He sounded very much like Bing Crosby. Yet, the artist whose signature song my dad loved and sang over and over again was Frank Sinatra's *My Way*. My dad was a true individualist and original. This was one of the greatest gifts he gave to me. I have tried to live my life 'my way' as he lived his.

On December 20th, 1974, my father and youngest sister Ivy, who was sixteen, died in a plane crash on their way to meet my mother who was waiting for them in Florida. Investigators concluded that an air traffic controller made mistakes in information given to my father.

My dad's legacy lives on through his daughters. There is not a day that goes by in which we are not inspired and motivated by my father's philosophy of living and loving. My dad lived it his way.

FOUR SISTERS IN LIFE AND DEATH

I believe in Ivy. She is my youngest sister. She died in a plane crash with my father when she was sixteen.

Ivy was born an old soul. There was something in her brown eyes that touched your core when she looked at you. When she smiled, you knew that she understood.

I lived at home for most of Ivy's life. That was my good fortune. Our bedrooms were next to one another. We shared a common wall. Every night when we went to sleep I would call out to her through the wall "good night, love-love. Sweet dreams."

That was my nickname for her. *Love-love* described how I felt about her. It was a double love. We were thirteen years apart. She was my youngest sister and the daughter I would have wanted.

When Ivy was in high school, her English teacher wanted to promote her into Honors English. As was her style, she asked the family's advice, pondered it, and then came up with her own practical and clear decision.

On this issue she had decided to stay in regular level English because she felt that her teacher was excellent. She said that when he spoke, he made her want to "hug a dictionary." Ivy was fourteen years old at the time of this particular insight.

She was the girl who befriended the underdog. If someone was made fun of by the group, Ivy would defend that person and protect his or her feelings. Her friends were a cross-section of many different types of people.

Ivy was quiet and gentle. Often she would observe others not missing a thing. She was thoughtful, endearing, and loyal. She was her own person, her own young woman. Unknowingly she had no time to waste. She had only sixteen years to do what she was going to do.

Ivy observed that there were many people who were quietly giving of themselves but who were never noticed or acknowledged for their generosity of time and caring. After the plane crash, based on Ivy's philosophy, my family created The Ivy Lynn Chaplik Humanitarian Award at her high school.

Ivy's beauty lives on in her family's and friends' hearts. In the hearts of her award nominees each year, her being is once again touched and her beliefs continue to inspire.

I have been blessed with three sisters: Linda, Susan, and Ivy. They are my treasures. They come from the same love from which I came. We are bound by DNA. Yet we are also connected by an invisible frame and foundation in which and upon which our lives have been shaped and implemented.

What happens when one of the four sisters goes away? Dies? Devastation and longing continue always. And then the magic happens. The unspoken focus among the three of us to keep our Ivy with us in life. If someone speaks of the three of us, in an almost naturally choreographed oneness, we answer "four. And she was the best."

There will always be four. We are four. We exist as four. We loved and love as four. We are four sisters in life and in death.

TWICE IN ONE FAMILY

A few years after the commercial plane crash that killed my grandmother, my university creative writing Professor told me in his critique that I had the raw material for a masterpiece. I wonder what he would have added eleven years later when I lost my father and youngest sister in a private plane crash.

Welcome to my life. I often wish I was a writer of fiction. I would prefer to be writing from imagination than from memory.

February 12, 1963. Lincoln's birthday. No school. My mother, five-year-old sister Ivy, cousin Larry and I were headed to the airport in Chicago to pick up my grandmother who was returning from Florida. A few years after losing my grandfather, my family convinced my grandmother to take a vacation in Florida. She was with my mother and youngest sister Ivy at the beginning of her holiday. Before they left for home, my mother found a small hotel for seniors and my grandmother stayed on for twelve more days.

My beloved grandmother never made it home. The commercial plane she was on hit a squall during the first ten minutes it was in the air and crashed in the Florida Everglades. Everyone on board was killed. My grandmother was sixty-seven.

I can touch the raw agony of that day when we found out that we lost her like it was yesterday. I was seventeen and about to graduate from high school and head to college in the fall.

We were assured her death was quick but I will never really know if she had time to be afraid. That question tortures me when I allow myself to think about it.

1963 was the year of the Cuban Missile Crisis. United States planes were being hijacked to Cuba. When my family and I reached the reservation desk at O'Hare airport, my mother looked up at the departure and arrival screen and read aloud. She found my grandmother's plane number but there was no arrival time listed. When she finished reading the information, we turned to our left and saw a man with what looked like a motion picture camera pointed our way. In unison we turned to the right to see if he was filming a celebrity but there was no one there. Realizing that he was filming us, my mother started screaming "the plane, the plane."

Suddenly airport personnel surrounded us and ushered us to a room on the airport's second floor. This room was filled with the families and friends who had passengers on my grandmother's flight.

"Go call daddy," my mother was crying. I bolted out of that room with my cousin Larry and headed to the main floor searching for a phone booth. My call to my father was interrupted by reporters who had spotted us and had descended on us like vultures.

"You and the little boy. Look toward the cameras," they were shouting. Larry started to cry.

"Leave us alone," I shouted back.

The airline did not confirm what they already knew about the plane's fate, making us and the other families wait for several hours. We actually were hoping the plane had been hijacked and that the passengers were all safely on the ground in Cuba. When the news finally was delivered to us, we were numb. My mother sat staring into space, her face tear stained, her eyes swollen red. Every few moments someone in that room would moan, start to rock, and then burst into tears. The agony in the room was palpable. We had bonded in a hell of our own.

My father had earned his private pilot's license years before my grandmother's plane crash. He loved flying. After the accident, he gave it up for my mother's peace of mind.

Years later my mother could see and feel my father's longing to return to the sky. She gave him her blessing to go back to his passionate avocation. My father was a Renaissance man. He was meticulous and quite brilliant.

December 20, 1974. The holidays were about to begin. My father and sister Ivy were flying in my father's plane to our vacation home in Florida. My mother was already there waiting for them with my cousin Larry who was visiting. I was planning to join them the following day and would be flying commercially.

As I walked into my apartment after work, my phone was ringing. My sister Linda's voice was quivering and desperate.

"There has been an accident. We are trying to find out details."

I froze. This was the second time I had heard this gut wrenching scenario. Reacting, I raised my arm and brought it down with such force that I smashed the face of my watch against my table. I wore that cracked face of my watch for years because it represented what I felt like inside.

In Florida, waiting for my father and sister who were late to arrive, my mother was making phone calls from her end as well. She finally reached the airport and was told there had been an accident.

"What hospital are they in?" she pleaded. There was a long pause on the other end and then the words "I am so sorry. The report does not read that way."

My mother and Larry started screaming. There was no way this could be happening. Her husband and sixteen year old daughter. This was not possible. Not again.

We were told from investigators whom we hired that there had been errors on the part of the air controller who was in communication with my father's plane.

We could not bear it and chose not to see them in their caskets. For months after the accident, whenever our doorbell rang, we thought that it was my father and Ivy coming home. It had all been a terrible mistake. They found their way back to us.

For years I have had the same dream of Ivy returning. I ask her where she has been, genuinely not knowing what has happened. She always smiles and does not answer. Then we embrace. Her hug is a homecoming. I never want to let go of her. I do not want to wake and know this is a dream.

I wish this was fiction.

Two

Living and Laughing through Middle Age

THE NEEDLE IN THE HAYSTACK

The odds were nothing less than finding a needle in a haystack. Richard was a forty-nine year old man. I was a forty-two year old woman. Our search for the needle was about to end on a dance floor. Across a dark crowded room Richard saw me first. I was dancing and as the other dancers moved making a slight opening, I saw him for the first time. He was smiling as our eyes met. I smiled back, the dancers again shifted their fluid form, and he was gone from view.

When the dancing ended, I walked toward the man with the welcoming face. Standing in front of one another, we made our introductions and acknowledged the like coincidences of our professions and educational backgrounds.

Richard joined me on the dance floor. Dancing was my passion not his. Yet he kept up with me. We closed the club. We were strangers in the night like Sinatra's song.

Two nights later we shared a walk and talked about our pasts and our dreams of finding a needle in a haystack. We held hands and hoped our search had possibly ended.

Could we have defied the odds of the single world? Could one glance in a crowded dance club have changed the course of our lives? We were not singles in our twenties or thirties. I was one month into my forty-second year. Richard was four months away from turning fifty.

This prince charming and his princess were on the brink of middle age. The needle was harder to see and more difficult to thread. We were acutely aware of the golden chance dancing had brought us that night.

Richard visited me every night the week after we met. I liked him in a way I had never felt about anyone before. He was a man comfortable in his own skin. He was real. There was nothing phony about him. His gentleness was so appealing to me. We were beginning an exploration of us but our search for the one-in-a-million needle was over.

As Richard tells it, and he tells it correctly, I made him wait two years before I agreed to marry him. It wasn't, however, him whom I questioned. It was the decision to marry. I was a professional woman with a dynamic and fulfilling career. My friends were loyal. My freedom was valued. It was difficult for me as a single woman in my forties to think of sharing my personal space with another. My thinking at the time went something like this. If I married, Richard would live with me. He would be there all the time. All the time! How and when would I have my cherished privacy?

It took me two years to work through this fear. During that time Richard was not only my lover. He was becoming my best friend. That was the key to our successful growth as a couple. He was my friend and I was his. When I felt closed in by our relationship, I talked to him about it. When I wondered what it would be like to share my space, I talked to him about it. When I hungered for my freedom, I talked to him about it.

One day I told Richard that I was going to attend a singles party. I felt like once again seeing what it was like. We had been dating for several months at that point and I was restless. He looked at me for what seemed like a long time and then he told me that if that was what I needed to do I should do it. He said that he was not happy about it but I was free to make that decision. I told him that I would not do anything behind his back and that I intended to go.

A few nights later I walked into the party. During my first hour there a number of men approached me and asked if I would like a drink or if I would like to dance. I continually answered no. As I walked through the room, I started wondering why I was there. Then I started missing Richard. I missed the familiar ease and gentleness of our connection. I missed his face. I missed him.

I left the party, which was downtown, got into my car and drove to Richard's house, which was in a Chicago suburb. I knocked on the door. He opened it and extended his arms toward me. "I was hoping and waiting," he said softly. We stood there hugging for what seemed like forever.

What happened that night was a turning point in our relationship. I was beginning to realize that I wanted us. Yet I still wasn't sure how it would all work. We each had our own long standing phone numbers, checkbooks and saving accounts. We each had treasured furniture and favorite colors and specific ways of doing things. In reality as small as these issues may have been, we were two people with established lives. I was used to being single. If I wanted cereal for dinner, I would have it. If I wanted to take a bubble bath at one in the morning, I did it. I had been living my life in single mode for a very, very long time.

Once I admitted to myself that my life was more fulfilling because I shared it with Richard, we worked through the logistics of our separate lives and set our wedding date.

The day I married Richard was the day before my forty-fourth birthday. We walked down our wedding aisle together because for us that was a symbol of how we felt about our life as a couple. We had grown into a partnership of equality and sharing. This was all I could ask. This was all I ever wanted in a relationship. I took his last name and kept mine. My hyphenated name became an everyday reminder of my pride in being me and in being Richard's wife.

As the years have passed, Richard's arms have become my home. My space has become our space. If Richard is not with me in it, I miss him. When I need privacy, I take it and my husband understands. What I feared has long ago left me. What has evolved is a union of two souls that has formed a oneness that retains the essence of who we both are as individuals. We are a man and a woman. We are a husband and wife.

We are a reality I was once afraid to dream.

Richard does not let me forget that I made him wait two years. I, however, am a believer that one cannot be what one needs to be until one is ready. Richard refers to our relationship as timeless love.

We often tell each other the story of a man who saw a woman dancing and wanted to meet her. We know that we both found the needle in the haystack.

RONALD

June 18th was our wedding day. Richard and I were driven to the synagogue where our ceremony would take place. The setting was breathtaking. The temple was situated on acres of green landscape. The synagogue was designed by a Japanese architect. It was all white with a form and shape of simple elegance and grace.

Richard was fifty-one and I was forty-three when we married. I chose to walk down the aisle hand in hand with my future husband at my side. That was the way I wanted to start our life together as partners.

I remember smiling at our guests as we walked toward the Rabbi. Everyone there meant so much to us. They smiled back at us with the recognition of how special a moment this was in our lives. We had waited a long time for this day. It was going to be perfect.

When the ceremony was over, the guests cornered us to extend their congratulations. My sisters somehow broke away from the crowd and walked into the room where tables were set up for our reception.

They gasped at the beauty of the peach colored roses and matching tablecloths and napkins. My sister Susan walked over to one of the tables and picked up one of the scripted napkins. She stared at the names and froze.

"Linda, come here," she called out to my sister. "The napkins say Elynne and *Ronald*."

"Very funny," Linda answered as she walked toward Susan and the napkin. Taking the napkin from Susan's hands she looked at the names and screamed. "Hurry! Pick up all the napkins on every table!"

While my new husband Richard and I continued greeting our guests in another part of the synagogue, my sisters worked as fast as they could to remove the disaster awaiting us. They tried their hardest but missed a couple tables. As fate would have it this is where Richard's friends sat down to eat. They looked at the napkins in total disbelief. One of his friends told us years later that she thought all the time she had known Richard she must not have known that his real name was Ronald.

On our honeymoon I could not resist every now and then calling for Ronald.

HONEY, BELIEVE ME

It seemed like a perfect plan. For our honeymoon Richard and I would combine two of our favorite places on earth, Bermuda and New England. We were marrying at the ages of fifty-one and forty-three. This was my first marriage. Before we had met, we had both traveled extensively. Our honeymoon was the beginning of our uniting the *us* we had waited for and anticipated.

I had vacationed alone in Bermuda where I would explore the island for hours by motor scooter. When we agreed upon our honeymoon itinerary, I was so excited to share my love of this island with my groom. I envisioned Richard riding at my side along Bermuda's glistening blue water. This was one of the most beautiful places I had ever seen in my worldwide travels.

For me there was no better way to see the island than by motor scooter. The sense of freedom and the thrill of the ride were incomparable to any way I had traveled.

The first day of our honeymoon I boarded my scooter like a pro. I had learned to wear gloves even though it was summer. I would grip the handles tightly because one had to concentrate hard. Bermuda only had one road with two lanes and used the English method of road travel. The directions of the lanes were the opposite of what we drove in the States. One would see tourists either limping on crutches or wearing a t- shirt that said *I survived the Bermuda Triangle.*

Getting on his scooter, Richard was tentative, this being a new experience for him. He drove behind me. Although I am a speed demon, I tried to go at a slower pace looking back every now and then to make sure he was still with me. This was not exactly the fantasy I had envisioned, but I was grateful to my new husband for making the attempt to join me in the way I loved to travel.

We stopped to visit a factory where perfume was made from the island's wild flowers. It was a glorious tour, both fascinating and sweet smelling. When we returned to the parking lot, we got on our motorbikes and I again took the lead. Enjoying the fresh air and colorful scenery, I finally turned my head to check on Richard. He was not behind me. I stopped and pulled over to wait for him thinking that I had been going too fast. Still no Richard. I turned around to backtrack. When I reached the perfume factory parking lot, I saw Richard talking to two other bikers. I thought how incredible that he might have met someone he knew. As I came closer, I realized that was not what had happened.

The exit to the parking lot curved. As Richard reached that point, he mistakenly pressed the gas pedal and accelerated. The bike went to the left and my groom flew to the right landing on a stone wall on his stomach. The other two bikers were passing by and stopped to rescue him. Luckily there was no heavy traffic.

Once we returned to our hotel, my new husband refused to attempt another ride and has never since been on a motorbike.

With his bruised ribs, we were off to New England, his honeymoon destination choice. This time he insisted we tour by car. We arrived at The Inn at Saw Mill Farm in Vermont. We were booked to stay in one of the Inn's rustic cabins. We took our bags inside and smiled at one another as we saw the two level structure and décor. The bedroom on the second level looked cozy. This was honeymoon perfect.

We walked outside to our private patio deck overlooking the lake. The setting was breathtaking with greenery and water everywhere. Richard put his arm around my shoulders and stepped toward me. He was still in pain from his Bermuda mishap. Suddenly as he stepped closer, I felt him going down. He grabbed my shoulders tighter to try to keep his balance. His leg had gone through a rotten floor plank. I turned and threw my arms around him trying to keep him from falling. If he had not been holding on to me, he would have torn something that would have ended the honeymoon.

"Honey, I am really not trying to kill you on our honeymoon," I said as we both started laughing uncontrollably. "Honey, please believe me."

A VALENTINE STORY

My husband knew what Valentine's Day meant to me. He bought me a touching Valentine card, ordered my favorite yellow roses and planned our evening at a new supper club in Chicago that we read had a live band and Sinatra slow dancing music. He booked the dinner a month in advance and requested the main floor of the bi-level restaurant.

Two weeks prior to February 14th Richard and I both came down with horrid sinus colds. All we could think about was that we had to be well for our slow dancing dinner date. I stayed in as much as I could trying to baby the worst cold I ever had.

We were not free of the congestion on February 14th, but it would not stop us. We were going to celebrate.

Richard wore his new pin striped gray suite and I wore my lavender velvet blazer with a pink sweater and my dancer's pin. We called a cab and excitedly anticipated our evening during the fifteen-minute drive to the restaurant.

Our reservation was at 7 pm. When we walked in, we were taken to a table that was close to the noisy bar. Staring at a dining room of mostly empty tables, we asked to be seated in a more conducive part of the room. One would think we had asked for the keys to the restaurant. The complexity of moving us from one empty table to another required a meeting between the hostess and the manager. They tried to place us in the balcony but it lacked the ambiance of the larger dining room so we refused table number two.

The manager offered to give us a corner table in the main dining room. It was a table for two next to a curtain. I should have known. As we picked up our menus, the clatter of servers' trays and banging from the swinging kitchen doors on the other side of the curtain made me jump. We were having our romantic Valentine's dinner in what sounded and felt like a construction zone.

Back I went to the manager who informed me that he had moved us three times. I informed him that this was a special night for us and if he would give us one of the empty tables with a better location I would be grateful. Again he stated that he had moved us three times. Before I turned to return to our table behind the curtain that led to door number one, the kitchen, I informed the pompous manager that my husband would be reviewing his restaurant. Richard's Restaurant Reviews had a following among Chicago business people. I wanted everyone to know about this place.

Each time the kitchen door swung open it banged into something on the other side of the curtain next to us and I jumped. It jarred my insides. We tried to change our focus and asked our server when the live slow dance music would begin. She told us 9 pm. I explained that I had been told 8 pm. She corrected me and explained that on weekends the music started at 9. The manager had also told me that we had one and one half hours to keep our table. Although math was not my strong point, I quickly realized that the dancing would start without our having a table.

We decided to order dinner. I continued to jump every time the doors and trays on the other side of the curtain banged into one another.

Richard and I both ordered the Tilapia. We loved Tilapia. How could anyone ruin Tilapia? This restaurant did. It was tasteless. I had to beg Richard not to offer to show the chef how to cook it. He settled on asking for garlic powder at our table.

When we finished what we could eat of our fish, I reminded Richard to take his calcium. Richard hates taking the large calcium pills yet he calmly told me that they were the best part of his dinner.

My cold had left me with a cold sore above my lip that I had kept moist trying to help it heal. For my evening out, I had to use cover up make-up that in just a couple of hours had dried and cracked the wound. I told Richard that it really hurt and that I had nothing with me to soothe it. He leaned toward me and told me to use the olive oil on the table. I burst out laughing at the ridiculous suggestion. Then out of desperation I did it. The pain stopped.

The service was so slow that there was no problem still having our table at 9. I told Richard that I thought the musicians would soon be setting up. He excused himself to go to the bathroom and when he returned he told me that there was only one pianist with percussion symbols that he seemed to control with his foot. There was no band. This was nothing more than a piano bar with a postage stamp dance floor.

When the server brought the dessert menu, she told us that our desserts were on the house. I had gotten to the manager after all. He cared enough to give us free desserts because my husband was reviewing his restaurant but not enough to give us a table away from the combat zone. When the server brought us the bill, Richard asked her what other work she did. She told us she was in school preparing to go into medicine. She said that she had no desire to work on live people once she became a doctor. She loved the sanctity of dead bodies and wanted to be a forensic pathologist. My husband seemed genuinely interested in this dinner conversation. I moved to kick him under the table. I was becoming desperate to discretely apply more olive oil to my wound.

After dessert the pianist started playing music that we had no desire to dance to with a singer we had no desire to hear so we left. We found a cab and returned home by 10pm. Richard put on our love song "Strangers in the Night" and we slow danced to Sinatra in our apartment overlooking Chicago's exquisite skyline.

We removed our Valentine fineries and retreated to our computers where Richard started writing his restaurant review and I began writing our evening's Valentine story.

THE HOTEL BALCONY

It was our annual theater trip to New York, my favorite city in the world. The taxi pulled up in front of our hotel located on 54th Street. We checked in at the front desk, got the keys to our one bedroom suite and headed to the elevator. It was midnight and we were exhausted from a day of airport traveling and delays.

We entered our room and I immediately started to unpack. About an hour later we were ready to go to sleep. My husband walked to his usual side of the king bed and I walked to mine. We climbed into bed and suddenly with a great force we both rolled to the middle of the bed crashing into one another. For a moment we could not speak and just looked at one another.

"What happened?" my husband finally blurted out.

"I don't know," I answered. We tried to roll the other way toward the edges of the bed but neither of us could make it out. We kept rolling back to the middle and into one another. After several minutes of uncoordinated frustration we got out of the bed and stood looking at it.

"This bed is broken," my husband finally concluded. "Look at the frame. It has totally come apart."

I got on the phone and called the front desk. It was by now almost two in the morning. The night manager officiously informed me that the hotel was full and that we would have to wait for morning to change rooms. That news was not what we wanted to hear. I argued with him but got nowhere.

"Would you like us to sit up all night?" I asked in my most sarcastic tone.

He let me know that whether we used the broken bed or not was certainly our choice. We were livid.

I let my tired husband have the middle of the broken bed to himself and I took one of the overstuffed chairs. I did not need an alarm clock that morning. I was on the phone to the morning manager before she could have her first cup of coffee. She asked to come up and see the bed. That meant waking and moving my husband. I told her yes. He was not pleased.

"This bed is definitely broken," she declared.

"So is my back," my husband retorted.

I was too tired to comment.

"We will move you to another suite as soon as it is cleaned," she offered.

We nodded our acceptance. Because we were unpacked, I wanted to supervise the change of rooms. This was not the way I had hoped to spend my first vacation day in New York.

Finally settled in our second room, I walked into the bathroom. Sitting and looking around me I suddenly focused on the sink that had literally pulled away from the wall and was ready to fall.

"Oh honey," I calmly called to my husband. "Would you please come in here?"

"What is that?" he asked incredulously.

"Let me call our friend the morning manager," I responded.

"Oh this is very dangerous," she observed. She called for the yellow tape they use to block off crime scenes and proceeded to place it over the bathroom entrance.

Completely sleep deprived, at that moment I had had enough. "What are you going to do for us next?" I asked in my most desperate and determined voice.

"Mr. and Mrs. Aleskow, we would like to offer you the hotel apartment for the remainder of your stay," she answered apologetically.

I could see that my husband was beyond caring where his bed would be at this point. One of his least favorite things was having to change rooms. I on the other hand was intrigued by this new proposition.

The hotel apartment had one bedroom, a living room and dining room, and a balcony. It was lovely. The manager had us test the bed and handed us the keys.

We woke up Sunday morning, freshened up and walked out on our balcony overlooking Central Park on our right and Manhattan's office buildings on our left. My husband put his arm around my shoulders. I sensed a romantic moment about to happen when I felt his body suddenly freeze and tighten.

"Don't look, don't look," he whispered.

"Look at what?" I asked barely finishing my question before I saw the answer. From our rooftop balcony we were staring straight into an office building window with a man and woman having a great Sunday morning visit on a swivel chair. Not only was my husband whispering for some strange reason, but he was watching this X-rated scene focusing his head away from the sight and practically crossing his eyes to see it. He didn't want them to notice he was looking.

"I don't think they are aware of anything at this moment but their own pleasure," I assured him. Yet, he still would not turn his head toward them for fear of being discovered.

That afternoon we had a theater matinee. Nothing on Broadway could match the scene we watched from our hotel balcony that morning.

THE ROOM WITH NO ROOM

We could not wait. I had a story accepted for publication in an anthology titled *The Wisdom of Old Souls.* The editor and publisher of this book of stories about grandmothers were Canadian. My husband and I were invited to attend the book's launch in Kingston, Ontario. We would make it into a short vacation get-away.

Disgusted with airports and airplane travel's complexities, limitations and delays, Richard and I decided to book a sleeper on the train that would take us to Syracuse, New York. From there we would rent a car for the remaining two-hour drive to Kingston.

We were excited to go by train. There is a romantic essence to the leisure of train travel. My husband loves trains and enjoys boyhood memories of his train experiences.

We packed for this trip without the need to use plastic bags and to adhere to three-ounce bottle requirements. We were free to pack the way we did before Sept. 11th changed our air travel rules. These regulations had not yet reached Amtrak's boundaries.

We were taking a night train that would leave at 10pm. For the sleeper guests, there would be wine and cheese available in the dining car. The entire scenario sounded charming, something we no longer felt about flying.

We boarded about 9:45pm and with our luggage we were delivered to our deluxe sleeper. The ticket for this accommodation was almost three times what a plane ticket cost for the privilege of seeing this country.

For that exorbitant price we had a tin can to sleep in. When the sleeper was opened, it butted against the sink. I asked our steward how we were supposed to enter the room. A thin man, he demonstrated standing sideways as he took a deep breath and gingerly squeezed his way into the tiny square space in front of the minute lavatory that doubled as a toilet and shower. This was smaller than the airplane lavatories. The thought that anyone would want to shower in a toilet still confounds me.

My husband and I were dumbfounded. There was no way we both could stand at the same time. We had to negotiate each movement. The door to the toilet could only partially open because of our luggage. We thought we were clever keeping it with us thereby avoiding wait time at the end of the trip.

Richard and I climbed into the lower bunk. We were like a human jigsaw puzzle trying to fit our elbows and knees into the cramped space we shared. Why did we not use the upper bunk? Because we could not fit the ladder into the space with our luggage.

Throughout the night we drifted on and off but never really slept. There just was no room to fit together let alone sleep. Even the second Dramamine I took did not knock me out as I had hoped it would. I was just thankful that it kept me from getting motion sickness. I could have never survived that train ride without it. The jerky movements of the train were almost violent.

"This track needs work," my exhausted husband whispered. "And this space is not fit for humans."

That comment started me laughing uncontrollably.

Whenever Richard had to use the toilet, I had to get up sideways, move past the sink to the tiny open space in front of the toilet door, and sit down on the end of the bunk so Richard could squeeze into the toilet. Watching him try to fit through the slightly open door, I again became hysterical. He barely made it. We were constantly sucking in our stomachs to move. Anyone suffering claustrophobia would have never survived.

The explanation given to us for such narrow quarters was that this particular train had to go through tunnels. The entire layout including corridors and sleepers was cramped to put it politely. We were not the only ones complaining. Those passengers who were not in accommodations delusionally called deluxe literally spent their night and day in a cracker box.

When we reached our destination, I tried to get a refund for the return ticket. We would have rather gone home by any other mode of transportation. It was too late to get a refund so we were doomed to this hellhole. Richard was even willing to exchange our sleeper for coach seats. He thought traveling all night that way would be more comfortable. No switch.

Coming back we checked our luggage through to Chicago hoping that this would give us inches of extra space. When we walked into the sleeper compartment, there was no chair. We were told that a chair was being added to the sleepers one at a time. This was most unfortunate for me because as a motion sickness sufferer, I had to sit facing the way the train was going. The chair we did not have would have faced the way the train was going.

Without our luggage filling the tiny open corner of space in front of the toilet/shower, we were able to use the ladder. Richard gallantly climbed to the top bunk. I could hear him muttering about the train. In between my swallowing Dramamine, I was laughing.

"How can anyone sleep with that whistle blowing every few minutes?" were among his desperate musings in between trying to descend the ladder without falling on his way to the toilet/shower.

Breakfast was called for 6:00am. We had a wake-up call scheduled that we never needed. At 5:50 Richard and I were sitting in the dark in the dining room waiting for the lights to be turned on and breakfast to be served. Fortunately I was facing the way the train was moving and could eat.

When the train made a stop at 6:30 am and some passengers disembarked, Richard and I almost literally pressed our noses to the window. We waved good-bye and wished it was our time to get off the train.

SLIPPERY AND WATERLESS IN MADRID

My husband was adamant about his decision. He said that he was tired of using so much space for underwear in packing for travel. For our trip to Spain he intended to pack four pieces of nylon underpants and four undershirts that he would hand wash each night. I stressed the part about him washing his packing choices to make sure we were clear on that point. He nodded agreement. We zipped the luggage and were off for the airport.

This was our first trip to Spain. We had very close friends in Madrid who were looking forward to giving us a personal guided tour.

As fate would have it, the Chicago Bulls were playing their championship game the first night we were in Madrid. When we awoke in the morning, I went down to the front desk to see if anyone could tell me if they had won.

"Excuse me," I said to the young man behind the desk. "Can you tell me please how the Bulls did last night?"

"The boolz?" he asked looking at me rather puzzled.

It was at that moment that I realized I was an American asking how bulls were doing in Spain. I tried to hide my embarrassment.

"Michael Jordan Bulls," I responded shyly.

"Oh, Michael Jordan," the clerk repeated. "He win!"

I headed back to our room to tell my husband the great news. Our friends were going to pick us up in an hour. We had to quickly go to the supermercado so that we could get some bottled water. Because his back was hurting him, Richard had put on his nylon back brace. We walked as fast as we could. Walking down the aisles of the supermercado in search of water was an entertaining experience. We always enjoyed looking at another country's products and how they were displayed.

We found the water. I asked Richard for money because he was wearing the money belt. I watched my husband put his hand under his shirt searching for the money belt. As I watched, suddenly his hand moved down the inside of his trousers. He kept turning to try to find some privacy surrounded by shoppers selecting their vegetables. His hand went lower and he looked panicked.

"Honey, what are you doing?" I asked frantic that at any moment my husband would be arrested for improper public behavior.

"I can't find my money belt."

His answer was so desperate that I did not know whether I should laugh at what I was watching or cry because I was not going to be able to purchase water. By now every shopper around us was enjoying this private moment. Whatever they were selecting, they had stopped what they were doing and were focused on us.

When we returned to our hotel room and my husband undressed, we discovered that the money belt had slid down his thighs. His nylon underwear, his nylon brace and his nylon money belt were too slippery a combination. Luckily our friends brought extra bottled water for our Madrid tour that day.

UNEXPECTED

I am walking with my husband through a beautiful city. Rivers and canals are everywhere. Expansive green lush parks shade the bright glow of sunlight. Park benches are filled with people sitting and enjoying ice cream purchased from the myriad of ice cream street vendors. The afternoon is filled with splendor. Young couples are openly affectionate walking hand in hand and stopping for passionate kisses. People are smiling and seemingly carefree. Free is the operative word here for the city we are in is St. Petersburg, Russia. It is my birthday and our first day in this exquisite city.

We have come by train from Moscow where we spent four days walking this vibrant city with its contrast of old and new. The famous Moscow Gum Department Store has been replaced by a breathtaking shopping center. This influence of the West is startling among the Kremlin Towers and the Russian cathedrals with their astounding cupolas.

As we walk through the plaza of the Kremlin, we view an endless line of blue portable toilets lined up for public use. One of them has its door open with a matron sitting at a small desk inside. She has made this her office. This sight makes us laugh uncontrollably as we make our way to the Armory Palace. This is the oldest museum in the Kremlin filled with this country's overwhelming history. Seeing the incredibly stunning diamonds of the Czarinas makes me certain of what I would love for my birthday.

Although touring Moscow by foot is an invigorating experience with my bilingual husband, the beauty of St. Petersburg is awe-inspiring. The French architectural influence of St. Petersburg's buildings along with its canals and parks offers visitors an unexpected perception of color, beauty and joy. The expected grayness of the past lingers in fringe neighborhoods. The heart of the city and its streets shine.

Visiting Peterhof, the Summer Palace, is a fascinating day. Laughter fills the air with hidden water sprays and trick fountains throughout the grounds. Children and adults together try to outsmart the stones that initiate a waterfall soaking and cooling them on this hot summer day. When my husband quietly points to a man in the background whose sole job is to step on a pedal that initiates the water spray, I cannot stop laughing. All of these people are jumping back and forth on stones thinking that they are causing the water to spray when this man is doing it all with his foot. Peter the Great was a consummate practical joker who loved water tricks.

Visiting Russia during the White Nights in which there are twenty-three hours of daylight adds to the atmosphere of what we are experiencing. Streets are filled with people going to cafes and enjoying strolls well past midnight in bright light.

That my husband speaks fluent Russian is an invaluable advantage. We are welcomed warmly and suffer few if any of the typical travel frustrations because he speaks so well and is received by the people almost as one of their own. Some find it hard to believe that he was not born there.

The St. Petersburg metro stations are deep underground with three to five minute escalator rides that seem virtually endless. Going down the escalator is not unlike the sensation of an amusement park ride. The various metro stations are designed and decorated uniquely. Some have chandeliers and are decorated elegantly. It is an experience not to be missed.

This is my first trip to Russia and my husband Richard's third. The Russia of today as compared with what he experienced in the sixties is a very different physical entity. Socially, the people on the streets are more outgoing and relaxed. Crime, however, is still rampant and tourists are intended prey.

Since I first met my husband, he has told me of this land so far away. To accompany him is truly a profound joy. We have the gift of spending time with his relatives who live in St. Petersburg. And although we will not make the journey on this trip, the Ukraine is where both my paternal and maternal grandparents were born.

As Americans, both my husband and I have returned to our ancestral homeland. What we have found is an unexpected and enduring memory.

FIRST IN LINE

Finally the inspiration of where to go for a quick vacation get-away was decided. I booked reservations at the Polynesian Hotel, scheduled a flight, and we were off to Disney World.

We entered the park. Our eyes did not know where to focus first. We were so excited. Holding hands we strolled through Disney World stopping for favorite rides and exhibits as we roamed. The ice cream cones were the best.

This was everything we had heard about and more.

Mickey Mouse walked with us and Sleeping Beauty greeted us in a way that almost seemed spell like. This was fantasy in its purest form. Make-believe and pretend were the focus of the moment. Everywhere we looked there was something to see or to eat. Visitors were laughing and even crying babies seemed to be smiling at their surroundings.

Disney World had just invited Hollywood into its Magic Kingdom. We made sure we had time for that newest attraction.

Before we were about to take the movie studio tour, I told Richard that I had to use the ladies' room and to wait for me. I left him sitting on a bench near the ladies' room entrance.

When I came out, Richard was gone. I thought perhaps he had gone to the bathroom so I sat down on the bench to wait for him. I waited for quite a while before I got up and started pacing while calling his name at first in my normal volume. As time went on I walked further and was now calling out his name at the top of my lungs. People were looking at me with sympathy.

Suddenly a woman approached me, put her hand on my arm and in her most gentle and soothing voice asked me if I had lost Richard. I noticed her badge and realized she worked at the park.

"Yes," I answered almost in tears. "I have lost Richard." By now she had her arm around me and was gently rubbing my back.

"Don't worry. We will find Richard. Tell me please, how old is he?"

That question threw me. "He is fifty," I answered.

That answer threw her. "Fifty?"

"Yes, fifty, and when I find him ..."

"But I thought you lost your child," she said.

"No, just my husband," I answered.

"We will find him. Follow me."

She took me through an employee only door that led to a platform. Climbing to the top I scanned the crowd control maze of people in line waiting to enter the studio. There at the head of the line was my husband Richard.

Did he think he was saving a place for me? Did he expect me to say excuse me to over six hundred people in order to eventually reach him in line? And how was I supposed to know he was in line when I had asked him to wait for me on the bench?

The Disney employee took me through a short cut to my waiting husband.

My husband looked embarrassed but proud that he was first in line.

THE HOLIDAY DIARY

There is nothing like a car trip through Canada. This is nature at its finest. It was difficult leaving the hospitality of Victoria. This port town has a charm all its own. The pace is relaxed and the walks are well marked and welcoming.

We rented a car to head to Tofino a town in British Columbia that is a five-hour drive through winding mountain roads and forests. It was breathtaking.

We arrived at our lodge that is situated on a private beach on the ocean. Our room consisted of a sitting room, a bathroom with a hot tub, a bedroom with a picture window overlooking the beach and ocean, and two fireplaces. There was also a small balcony. Here we would spend our Chanukah together.

The romantic atmosphere of this setting was close to perfection. Other than walks on the beach and dinner, we rarely left our suite.

One morning as we were having our breakfast in front of the picture window, I looked toward the fireplace and noticed a book sitting on the mantle. I reached for the book and opened it. It was a diary written by travelers who had stayed in this room.

I started reading the first entry.

"My name is Jim. My wife and I are searching for the most beautiful places on earth to visit before I die. I have terminal cancer. We love this spot, this view, this room."

I started to cry. My husband asked me if I was OK. I began to read the entries of the diary to him.

The next writer began her thoughts. "Before I write about why I am here, I want to comment on what Jim wrote."

By now I had a box of Kleenex next to me and soon needed a second one.

Each story was more moving than the last. "We return here for each anniversary." "We are on our honeymoon." "He proposed to me in this room." "We come here to watch storms and to hold one another."

When I finished reading, my husband asked me, "Are you going to write in the diary?"

"Yes," I answered with a smile. I looked at my husband for a long time. With this man I had found the love for which I had searched. He was not only my husband but also my best friend with whom I shared everything in my life. I was so happy in this special place because I shared it with him.

The romantic intimacy of this room was ours at this moment in time and yet we were connected to all the couples that had been here before us and would be here after us. We were strangers who were family because this room and its memories belonged to each of us.

A TALE OF TWO VARDAS

I was fearless in my twenties and thirties. I traveled the world alone, loving the adventure and spontaneity of my single life.

Decisions were not absolutes. They were quests.

In 1970, I traveled to Israel. Jerusalem remains, in my mind, the most unique city I have ever visited. While in the Old City, I had the distinct feeling that, at any minute, God was going to put His hand on my shoulder and say "Welcome, Elynne."

One afternoon, I took the train from Jerusalem to Tel Aviv. I met a young woman named Varda, who was my age. She lived on a Kibbutz and invited me to visit her over the Shabbat weekend. The Kibbutz was Israel's collective farm community.

Being alone, I was happy to accept her invitation. She gave me careful directions and told me she would see me soon. She waved as she left the train.

Sitting across the aisle from me was an older gentleman who had overheard the conversation I had shared with Varda. When Varda left, he motioned me to come and sit beside him.

"You must not go to that Kibbutz," he warned looking me straight in the eye.

"Why?" I asked.

"It's dangerous. It's on the Lebanese border. Very dangerous."

I smiled and thanked him with the full intention of continuing my plan.

When I wrote my mother in Chicago, I left out his warning but told her I had met a lovely older man on the train. My mother told the family that only her single daughter would go to Israel and meet a Tevye like in *Fiddler on the Roof*.

That weekend, I followed Varda's directions and took the train to the stop for Kibbutz Gaaton. When I got off the train, there was land as far as I could see, a train track, a small bench and me. I sat down with my suitcase and waited. Nothing and no one were in sight. I sat there desperately hoping that Varda did not forget me. Suddenly, in the distance, I saw a truck driving in my direction and heard a voice with a distinct Israeli accent calling my name. Varda and her friends had stopped to get ice cream for the American.

At the Kibbutz, they showed me around and we had a late dinner. Then we all turned in for the night. The bathroom was an outhouse. I knew there would be no way I would get through the night without having to use it. I had just seen the movie Exodus and remembered the scene of the brutal killing of Karen when she was out walking alone near the border.

Sure enough, I woke in the middle of the night. I took the flashlight Varda left for me by my bed and prayed all the way to the toilet and back. I could not remember ever feeling that much fear.

The next day, I visited the children at their school and toured more of the Kibbutz. Varda and her friends spoke very little English and my Hebrew was limited to basic words. I could not even speak a sentence. Yet somehow we managed to communicate. Sitting around the fire in the evening, we tried to talk about our favorite books. I asked if anyone had read Antoine de Saint Exupery's *The Little Prince*, which, at that time in my life, was one of my greatest treasures. Varda's eyes lit up. She ran to her cabin and brought out *The Little Prince* in Hebrew. I was speechless. I was on the other side of the world and yet I felt, in that moment, that I was home.

After my visit with Varda at the Kibbutz, I became restless and felt homesick. I inquired about going home early to Chicago and was put on a wait list. I eventually got the earlier flight out. At home four days later, I woke to the news that my original TWA flight had been hijacked. My homesickness had made me lucky.

Varda and I corresponded for about a year. She sent me *The Little*

Prince in Hebrew and I sent her the book in English. Then we lost touch. Forty years later, I am in my sixth decade of life. I joined the social network, Facebook, recently and have been contacted by many friends and acquaintances from my past. It is a unique opportunity.

Looking at my bookshelf, I found myself staring at my copy of *The Little Prince* in Hebrew from Varda. I started wondering how she was. I looked at her inscription on the page. She had only signed Varda with no last name. I wondered if I might be able to find her through Facebook. I typed the name Varda into the search box and a listing of over five hundred Vardas came up. As I examined the list, I saw that about one hundred of them said Varda: Last Name, Country: Israel.

I began to type: *Are you the Varda I met on a train in 1970 and visited at Kibbutz Gaaton? We both loved The Little Prince.*

Looking at photographs of faces, I wondered could she be the one? It had been almost forty years and I did not remember her face. I copied and pasted these words over and over, my speed building with each name. Suddenly, a warning message from Facebook popped up. Its system misinterpreted me as a spammer due to the volume and speed with which I was sending messages. Facebook warned me. I was on a mission and paid no attention. I had to reach each Varda with the chance of finding mine. Suddenly, Facebook issued its last warning and froze my access to sending messages for twenty-four hours. I had been penalized and put in the corner. This action only made me more determined to complete my list.

When I resumed, however, I dutifully slowed down the pace of my inquiries. When I had finished, I started to get back answers from the Facebook Vardas of Israel.

"Sorry, no I am not your Varda."

"No. I am not the one but I love *The Little Prince*."

Then one of the Israeli Vardas responded: "Please tell me more about the Varda you are trying to find."

I told her my story. She and I started an e-mail correspondence. There was a seven hour difference between Chicago and Israel. As I was going to bed, Varda was waking up. I would wish her good morning as she wished me good night.

One morning, I woke to an e-mail from her that was titled *Wakeup ... Surprise ... Surprise ...* In her e-mail, Varda told me that she had called Kibbutz Gaaton and had tracked down the married last name of the Varda for whom I was searching. That Varda had moved to another Kibbutz. My new friend, Varda, drove to the Kibbutz and within ten minutes was standing in the dining room in front of Varda number one telling her the whole story of my search. She got her e-mail address for me and within moments from the time of my receiving that *Wake up ...Surprise* e-mail, I was in touch with *The Little Prince* Varda I had met on the train.

It was a very pleasant reunion and Varda e-mailed me a copy of the inscription I had written in the book I had gifted her forty years ago.

It was good to know that Varda was well and to have found her through the gracious efforts of my new friend. Somehow, in the darkness of the infinite internet universe, I clicked send and found the way to find my original Varda. And at that moment, we both came home to one another.

THE RITUAL

Watching my husband prepare to drink a cup of coffee is a mesmerizing ritual. If at home, in preparation of the brew, he mixes ice cubes with water and freshly ground coffee in the electric coffee pot. I am not a drinker of coffee or tea but the aroma of his creation is exquisite. He says the ice cubes are his secret.

The coffee must be poured into the cup only three quarters full so that there is plenty of room left for skim milk. It is Richard's pet peeve when he politely but firmly asks a restaurant server to make sure to leave room for his milk, and the coffee comes to the table filled to the brim of the cup.

His other obsession is that a restaurant has skim milk. Having gone through bypass surgery, Richard is insistent that his needs and those of other customers like him be respected.

Watching him pour the milk to the top of the cup, he then picks up one packet of sugar, preferably raw sugar, and holds the packet at the top shaking it for about thirty seconds until he is satisfied that all the sugar has sunk to the bottom. He then delicately and carefully opens the packet and gently pours it into the coffee cup with the appropriate amount of milk. He picks up a spoon with the grace of a surgeon holding his scalpel and begins to stir. The stirring must be left to right. Clockwise. Why? Because.

If he is given stir sticks instead of a spoon, he is outraged. He begins a ten minute diatribe on their uselessness in appropriately stirring coffee. They are a waste of his time and any other serious coffee drinker.

He then waits a few moments for the coffee to cool and slowly, lovingly takes his first sip. If we are at a restaurant, I wait for Richard to give his thumbs up. It is the tradition that is the culmination of our meal. Much like Ebert and Siskel, Richard's thumbs define the value of what he has just experienced.

Tea is Richard's favorite drink. When we registered for our wedding gifts, one guest told me there had been a mistake because my list had two tea pots, one white and the other black. I answered that there was no mistake. My husband puts loose tea in the black pot and water in the white pot. The milk and sugar follow the same pattern as well as the stirring.

Tea is a ritual as is coffee. I enjoy watching Richard prepare and consume his delicacies more than if I myself was drinking them.

THE PILLOW

It all happened so fast. My husband went for a check-up with a new internist. This very astute and caring doctor took the time to check my husband's new EKG with the one my husband took the year before which had been in his records. He took the time. He told Richard that he saw a slight change and wanted to check it out. An echo stress test was scheduled.

The doctor called that afternoon and told us Richard must have an angiogram. The results of that procedure indicated that bypass surgery was required. Just like that! The surgeon told us that Richard was the type of man he worried about because he had no symptoms. He said that one day he could have been exercising or walking down the street and it would have suddenly been all over.

The bypass surgery was scheduled for November 15th, 2006. That was the most frightening day of my life. My husband was the picture of health as I kissed him good luck and they rolled him into surgery. The next time I saw him in the ICU was a very different scenario. Anyone who has seen a loved one after bypass will understand. I do not think there was one area of his body that did not have tubes in it. He was swollen from the surgery. But he had come through it. He needed a quadruple bypass. The next days in Intensive Care were agonizing.

The patient has one reality of suffering and his loved one has another. Watching my husband go through the suffering of this entire ordeal ripped me apart as well. When he was transferred to the cardiac floor, I remained with him in the hospital for the remainder of his stay. I slept on a window seat, which doubled as a so-called bed for relatives who wanted to stay overnight. I was determined that I would not walk out the door of that hospital without my husband at my side.

One day a volunteer walked in holding a large red pillow that was shaped as a heart. The wording on the pillow said "Mended Hearts" with a picture of a heart with a jagged line running through it. This organization was made up of men and women who had gone through bypass surgery. It was necessary for a patient to hold a pillow when coughing in order to control the pain.

When we came home from the hospital days before my husband's birthday, I told him that I wanted to have a few family and friends over for a short time to share his birthday cake. He got tired very easily and I wanted him to be comfortable. He sat there that night holding his mended hearts pillow close to his chest to help with the pain.

Months later when Richard was in Rehab and doing quite well, I asked him if he would mind my putting the red pillow away because it did not go with the colors of our den. He looked at me for what seemed a long time and answered that although the color was not coordinated with our decor, that pillow reminded him of what he went through and survived. I never mentioned removing it again.

A year later, Richard got an excellent health check-up report from his cardiologist. What a different day that was a year later. To say that I am grateful to that internist, is the understatement of my lifetime. The red pillow sits prominently on our couch as a reminder of our infinite good luck and Richard's determination to live positively and stay well.

A WONDERFUL LIFE INDEED

As a Jewish family we celebrate Chanukah not Christmas. However, we are excited about everything that goes with this time of year. We love Christmas songs, holiday lights and decorations, beautiful Christmas trees and perhaps most of all, Christmas movies. I wait all year for Frank Capra's "It's A Wonderful Life". I tape the film so I can view it at my leisure during the holiday season. This season seems to sparkle with hope and appreciation of all in our lives that is, was and will be.

Even though my husband and I were going to meet friends for lunch, I put on the movie to sneak a few moments before we left. In the meantime, my husband took my car key down to our condo's garage to get the car ready.

Before I turned the movie off to go downstairs to the garage, I was watching the scene in which Uncle Billy loses the Building & Loan's cash deposit. When the bank teller asks him for the money, Billy starts to frantically search his pockets. He then desperately retraces his steps from the bank back to the Bailey B&L where he must tell George, his nephew who heads the business, what has happened. Without the money to be deposited, the Bailey family's Building & Loan will become bankrupt with legal ramifications. The story's main plot continues from this point.

Watching Uncle Billy panicking as he searches for the money is a painful scene. As I headed to our building's elevator, my thoughts were with this touching character and his dilemma.

When I walked into the garage, my husband Richard was not there waiting for me. I walked around the garage looking for him and then decided to sit down to wait. A few minutes later, Richard walked into the garage looking distracted.

"You will not believe what happened to me," he said to me almost breathless.

"I brought down our garbage bags and threw them in the bins. Then I walked to the lobby and chatted with some residents and the doorman. From there I headed to the garage and walked to your car when I realized that your key to the car which I had had was not in my hand. I frantically searched my pockets and then desperately retraced my steps back to the lobby where I asked if anyone had found a lost car key. When that produced nothing, I walked back to the garbage bins and stood there. With great embarrassment, I asked the maintenance man if he would empty all the bags in the bin and look for a key that might have fallen out of my hand. He did so and at the bottom of the bin something was shiny. It was your car key."

Looking at Richard as he told me a similar story to the one I had just watched, I felt compassion for him. My husband was luckier than Uncle Billy. I knew it would have been easier to explain lost money to George than my lost car key to me. A wonderful life indeed!

THE THREE F'S

"It's the three F's," my cousin the doctor said.

"The three F's?" I asked somehow knowing this was not going to be good.

"Female, fat and forty," he replied.

A great fortieth birthday present. I needed to have my gallbladder removed.

It had started one morning with an attack of pain that made me curl up into a ball. There was no position that would offer relief. During this attack my mother called and in response to my moaning, she told me to get out of bed and walk three miles to work.

"You need exercise! Walk it off!"

I was finally able to get dressed and following my mother's advice, walked to work where I promptly headed into the ladies' room, threw-up, turned around and took a cab home.

The surgeon was more on target when he informed me that I had stones and that my gallbladder had to come out. I insisted on scheduling my surgery for after my fortieth birthday bash. Stones would not stop my celebration. I was single, a lover of birthday parties, and the founding General Manager of WYCC-TV/PBS. I was Chicago's first female TV GM and the station's on-air spokesperson. Chicagoans lovingly referred to their second PBS affiliate as Channel 20.

The hospital where I had my surgery allowed family to stay with you while you were being prepared. I was lying on the gurney feeling no pain and flying high. I was entertaining my family with my medically induced humor when a nurse pulled back the curtain of the waiting area I was in and started wheeling me out.

"Ok, Mary. Let's say goodbye to our loved ones," she said softly as she began to roll me away.

"Wait!" my sister Linda shouted at the top of her voice register. "This is not Mary."

The nurse abruptly stopped, looked at my ID bracelet for the first time, saw that my name was Elynne and promptly returned me to my family. To this day I wonder what Mary was having removed.

When I was finally brought to the correct room for my operation, I was transferred to an operating table, positioned in a torturous pose, and had my hospital gown removed. Lying there naked, nervously waiting for this dreaded experience to begin, I was suddenly aware that a woman's face was inches from mine.

"Are you the Channel 20 lady?" the nurse asked me.

All I could imagine was that my gallbladder removal was going to be telecast to the city. Was there no such thing as privacy left in this world? Would she next be asking for my autograph?

"Go away," I wanted to say. "Leave me in peace!" But I smiled and answered, "Yes. I am."

"I love your station and enjoy your warmth with your audience. You are really good."

"Thanks," I whispered.

I desperately looked at a second nurse with a nonverbal plea to get this woman away from me. Somehow I was understood and it was not long before I was put under.

Whether I was being taped, I would never know. This was one performance I would never want to see or share.

The next morning the doctor came into my room, proudly showed me a bottle filled with my stones, and asked me if I would like them as a souvenir. I thanked him and said "no." I then suggested he offer them to my #1 nurse fan with my thanks for being a loyal audience viewer.

RG

I am a woman who focuses on what I have rather than what I do not have. Yet, there are moments, utterly private *what if* moments, that I have shared only with my husband.

We married late in life. Our blessing of meeting one another was like finding a needle in a haystack. This is my first marriage. I was forty–three years old when I walked down the aisle. The next day I turned forty-four. The miracle of becoming *us* is what we celebrated. Our gratitude for finding one another made us giddy. Marriage had never been a priority in my life until I met and fell in love with Richard who became not only my husband, but also my best friend.

My marriage and my careers in television, education and writing were my focus along with travel. Our life has been exciting, fulfilling and joyous. We have pursued our individual dreams and those dreams we have built together.

One night Richard and I began a discussion on what it would have been like to have had a child together.

"I would have wanted a son who looks just like you," I responded.

I have three sisters and had always wanted a brother. So, wanting a son was a natural response. I love buying men's clothing for my husband. I enjoy the styles and combinations. The thought of dressing a little boy in overalls and suits and ties makes me smile. And if he was built like my husband, he would in all probability wear childhood husky sizes which means there would be a delicious amount of boy to hug.

"What would we name him?" Richard asked me, smiling.

We sat for a long time, thinking in silence.

"How about Reid Gregory?" I asked.

"After my father Rubin and your father Gregory. We would call him RG."

This pleased Richard. He immediately went into a scenario of what it would sound like calling RG in for dinner. The sound of those precious initials was a tribute to both our fathers.

Our discussions continued every now and then referring to RG, the son we might have had. Our talks were not morose. They were discussions about one part of our life we would not have, but we were realistic, always putting it into a context of what we did have and our gratitude for our blessings which were abundant.

Sometimes we would talk about the world the children of today face and we both would acknowledge it was possible that not bringing a child into such chaos might have in some ways been a good thing. On the other hand, would RG have been someone who would have helped lessen this world's despair? Being a combination of the two of us, I would have hoped so.

As a woman, I would have enjoyed the challenge of raising a sensitive and responsible male. His father would have been an ideal model for him. I would have tried to teach him about self-esteem and would have used all my abilities to raise a man who respected himself and others. I would have enjoyed encouraging RG to learn what it means to be friends with women and to love well.

Recently, Richard and I purchased a statue for my sister and brother-in-law's garden. It is a life size boy in sneakers sitting holding a bottle filled with lit fireflies. The 'boy' sat in our apartment for a couple of days until the anniversary party when we would give our gift.

As I entered our living room where 'the boy' was placed and Richard was reading the paper, I heard myself call out "How are my boys doing?"

That is a question I never had the opportunity to ask in my life. It would have been an experience I would have loved to have had. Instead, my focus has remained on the students I have taught and hopefully have inspired. I taught my Communication course as *Life*

101 and tried to teach my students self-esteem and how to reach for their potential. While some people cherish their roses and tulips, I have my prize-winning garden of students, many of whom have stayed in touch. Each is unique and beautiful. I was their professor, not their parent, but the hundreds of students I have had the privilege of teaching will always belong to me and I to them.

I never had the opportunity to give birth and to teach RG how to live, but I am a woman who has focused on what I can do with what I have. In profound ways, we are all parents to the world in which we live.

Three

Surprises

BREAKFAST AT TIFFANY'S... ALMOST

Once upon a time there was a character in a movie who was a free spirit with a love of adventure and life. Her name was Holly Golightly and she was played by the deliciously charismatic Audrey Hepburn. Her character inspired my secret plan.

This movie had a magical effect on me. I was sixteen when I saw Breakfast at Tiffany's for the first time. By the time I took my first trip to New York, I had seen the film four times.

Of all the cities I have visited in the world, New York is my most favorite and precious. The city has an infinite rhythm of its own. The opportunities of what to do and see are endless. Day or night one can eat. There is always choice for entertainment. The city is alive. It is a life-force.

I love the anonymity of New York. There is a need I have for the quixotic sensibility New York offers me. I am renewed and inspired by my immersion into this city. One can experience any art form. It is a walking city filled with amazing neighborhoods, quaint groceries, delis, cabarets, music, museums, parks and the ultimate in theater, Broadway.

Being in the audience of a Broadway musical, I transcend the reality outside the theater building and am uplifted magically into the all-encompassing talent on stage. The actors play to me beyond their potential to the ultimate of their gifts. The productions are often works of art. To be in a Broadway audience is one of the most satisfying moments of my life. It is for me existence in another dimension.

My first trip to New York was liberating. During the day I visited Central Park and the pond where Holden Caulfield watched the ducks in Catcher in the Rye. I went to New York's museums and walked Fifth Avenue. I played at FAO Schwarz Toy Store. I awoke every morning in my own fairytale waiting to see what the day in this city would offer me.

Holly Golightly and I breathed New York in the same way. I inhaled its anticipation first feeling it in my toes as it worked its way up to my chest and made my brain almost light headed. Tonight was the night I would implement my plan. This was a private plan. I had shared it with no one. It was all mine. I was a romantic and I was fearless.

The theater performance I attended ended around ten forty-five. I walked through Times Square to one of New York's twenty-four hour markets and bought doughnuts and milk. Carrying this sweet treasure I made my way back to my hotel through the exiting theater crowds.

Back in my room, I waited until midnight. With my package in hand I headed toward Tiffany's on Fifth Avenue. The door to this jewelry store is recessed. In the darkness of the early morning I stepped into the doorway and put on my sunglasses that were almost identical to those Audrey Hepburn wore in the movie. I unwrapped my donut, opened my milk and proceeded to have breakfast at Tiffany's.

Suddenly I saw a male figure pass the door in which I was standing. Almost immediately he slowly walked backwards and stopped, staring at me. I could see him more clearly now and realized he was a police officer.

"What are you doing?" he asked in a thick New York accent.

"Having breakfast at Tiffany's, officer," I replied suddenly feeling self-conscious.

"Oh yea?" he responded totally unconvinced. "You should know better than soliciting here."

"Soliciting?" I repeated. "No, officer, you do not understand. I am having breakfast at Tiffany's. Audrey Hepburn?" I stammered. "The movie?"

He just looked at me and shook his head. "Move on," he said.

At that moment I hoped that he thought anyone wearing sunglasses and drinking milk in the middle of the night while standing in Tiffany's doorway must be a tourist.

He had unexpectedly interrupted my fantasy but I had done it. Like my favorite movie character I was in New York having breakfast at Tiffany's. It would always be a once upon a time moment for me.

DANCER'S LANE

I could not sleep for weeks waiting for the moment. It was actually embarrassing because I felt like I was a child again anticipating my birthday and the parties that were planned for me. Yet, I was anything but a child. I was about to dance my way into my sixtieth birthday. In preparation for my parties I went shopping for three very different outfits. The one thing they all had in common was that I saw them as me. The tailored look with a lavender tie and striped shirt; the long flowing skirt in soft earth tones with a low beaded top; and a white and brown silk pants suit. My public self was in sync with my private self. I was bursting with excitement because I believe that it only gets better for a woman with each decade. The reasons for this belief come from the blessing of time and how that time has been filled as the fabric of one's life.

My parties were planned for Friday night, Saturday morning and Sunday evening which was my actual birthday.

When I woke Friday morning I walked around my apartment on the thirty-fifth floor of my Chicago high-rise. I stood looking out at the city's breathtaking skyline and lake. This was my city where I was born and although I had traveled extensively, where I had lived my soon to be sixty years. The view from my window was high above the city with its gloriously fire orange sunrise. I smiled at the memories Chicago and I had shared.

My mind wandered back to my forty-second birthday when one month later to the day I met my husband. My girlfriend Sandy and I would go disco dancing on Sunday nights to a dance place called the Snuggery.

I was going out to disco dance in my forties, something I had never done in my twenties or thirties. I had never gone the single bar scene. Yet now in my fourth decade I was enjoying one of my greatest passions. And it was the love of dancing that was about to change my life.

This particular Sunday evening Sandy was out of town so I went myself. A man asked me to dance and while we were on the stage, I looked out into the room and as the sea of dancers parted for a moment, I saw a face looking my way literally across a crowded room. The dancing bodies closed rank and the face was gone. Again, with people's movements, there he was, smiling at me. I thought what a great face and when the dance was over, I walked over to meet Richard. I did not know that for the first time I had just seen the man whom I would marry.

Richard was a classical music lover. He had been talked into going dancing by some of his friends. He valiantly kept up with me on the dance floor although this was not really his choice of leisure entertainment. Yet something had clearly happened between us. We closed the Snuggery that night. This was his first and last time in a disco.

That my husband and I share the ultimate friendship is the timeless love of my existence. As a newlywed for the first time at age forty-three, the many perspectives awaiting me were unknowns at the time I made my decision to marry. I was terrified. A full career, social life and valued freedom kept me content and even happy.

I did not know, when I finally accepted the idea of marriage, that I was about to become a partner in an existence far beyond my present life, my dreams of loving, my hope of sharing in equality.

I have been blessed with a life partner in marriage who with ease, grace and natural inclination makes me feel my personal and professional being fits with his essence as a human, a husband, a lover, a friend.

In this time of single life complexities and egos, it is not something I take for granted that I have a relationship that fulfills my potential and sense of completeness.

That Richard and I have found and continue to develop our loving is a simple truth; that we were able to do this without the struggles and confusions of a contemporary woman and man is due to real luck, consistent appreciation and an intangible link between us. We are a man and a woman; we are individuals.

As husband and wife, we have become not less than we were as singles, but what we always were and more. The more is something I knew nothing of even in imagination. It is something that has been created by forming a oneness that retains the breadth and height of two souls and minds.

As I stood at the window remembering and thinking these thoughts, I suddenly was aware that many of my out-of-town friends would be flying in within the next few hours for my weekend. Richard had arranged for a white limousine to take us to the Friday night party.

My sisters had planned an all-women's dancing party for me. My lavender tie outfit with pants and white blazer made me feel as close to Travolta as I possibly could. Tonight I was Travolta and more.

My sisters gave me a magical sixtieth birthday party. On the dance floor the women I loved and admired surrounded me in a circle. I danced in the center to Gretchen Cryer's song *Happy Birthday* from her play *I Am Getting My Act Together And Taking It On The Road*. They sang with Gretchen's voice as I danced in celebration. I was profoundly with them but at the same time I was in my own joyous solitude. I was transcended into a place deep within myself where I live and love and write and feel and share and dance.

I wanted a dancing party. This was the way I could express the magical freedom I was feeling. It was more than a birthday I was celebrating. It was living sixty years and all the blessings in that time. And as a woman it was coming through five decades to my sixth which was somehow liberating and satisfying and hopeful.

Had I spent my life well? Had my first five decades shared the love I felt, the inspiration I had hoped I offered, the personal and professional vision to which I had aspired, the legacy I had hoped I was creating?

The next morning the out-of-towners, my family and our couples friends shared a birthday brunch hosted by my husband Richard.

He had the restaurant's dining room decorated with five hundred balloons of every color of the rainbow. It was my fantasy.

Around the table he had cards tied with bows. Each card stated what I was in my life: Professor, author, wife, best friend, daughter, sister, TV manager and on-air spokesperson. My husband's loving blue eyes smiled at his accomplishment in making this warm and glowing celebration for me. And what made the day especially grand was that it was also our 16th wedding anniversary.

On Sunday I awoke to my sixtieth year and an elegant intimate dinner party my mother gave for me that evening.

What a welcome to my sixth decade. Six is a blessed number. It is the family unit from which I began as the eldest of four sisters. It is a time that belongs to me and the man I love. It is a time for new dreams and action. It is a time for celebration and thanks. I am filled with gratitude and hope. And I am dancing.

THE REVOLVING DOOR

I have had a weight problem since I was a child. One of my closest and most cherished friends is chocolate. Even pronouncing the word makes me salivate. Chocolate has been a pure, constant and delicious companion.

My sisters and I all battle the scale. Sugar is our nemesis. My sister Linda and I have an ongoing joke that we have never been thin at the same time. We are always giving each other pep talks about losing weight. We try our hardest to motivate one another without creating resentment for interference with our beloved chocolate.

One winter morning I got on the scale and wept. How did the number I was staring at happen? I swore that I would start my diet that day and would give up chocolate until I reached my goal. To seemingly guarantee my promise to myself, I called Linda and said it aloud to her. Now it was real and that made it scary.

To my surprise four weeks passed and I had not once cheated. I worked downtown and decided one day to do some errands. As I was walking down the main boulevard of Chicago, I suddenly looked up and realized that I was standing and waiting for the traffic light to change in front of a Fannie May Candy Store. This was my favorite chocolate in the world next to Cadbury.

As I looked in the window at the display of boxes filled with chocolate butter creams, turtles and fudge, my knees started to buckle. I almost had to hold on to the side of the building. I could feel my resolve dissolving. *One month* I kept saying to myself. *You have gone without chocolate for one month. Keep walking. Cross the street. Now.*

I was not listening. The imagined taste of the chocolate on my tongue had taken over. My brain had disengaged. Only my taste buds were operating in anticipation of what I was about to do.

I walked to the store's revolving door and entered it. I pushed hard to make the door go as fast as I could. As the door swung into the store I was ready to disembark toward the candy counter when I realized that I could not stop revolving and therefore could not enter the store. Somehow the door kept going until I was again outside on the street. I looked up in shock to see my sister Linda behind me pushing that door with all her strength. I had pushed myself into the store and she had pushed me out.

Linda happened to be passing by at the moment I weakened. She saw me start my journey toward chocolate and moved as quickly as she could to save me. And she did. We laughed so hard that my need for a chocolate fix passed for the moment. The next craving was an absolute surety. The question was not if but when and where would Linda be when I needed her!

PLEASE BE ANONYMOUS

My sister Linda and I each separately went into the bathroom we shared with our other two sisters. We had to weigh ourselves before we left the house on our dreaded journey. We would allow ourselves to be tortured before we would divulge our weight. When I celebrated my sixteenth birthday, the number of pounds on my driver's license was what I weighed when I was fourteen. I would not change that number until I had to make up a new number when I turned twenty-one.

Linda and I were desperate. We were sugar addicts who wanted to be thin. We tried every diet imaginable. On the newest fad liquid diet that had women watching pounds melt away, I gained weight. I cried all day after weighing myself, having been totally committed for one week to liquids for two meals and a healthy dinner. Linda struggled as well on frozen dinner diets. Nothing worked for us in the end because even if we lost a few pounds, we eventually succumbed to binging on our favorite sugar treats. And for some reason, the universe would never allow both of us to be successful in dieting at the same time.

One day Linda and I had a heart-to-heart. I could barely say my thought out loud.

"I have read about something. I am not sure we will have the courage to do it but I don't know what else we can try."

Linda was cautiously watching my facial expressions as I spoke.

"Have you ever heard of Overeaters Anonymous?" I barely whispered.

"Yes," Linda replied in an even softer volume. She lowered her eyes. I thought she was going to cry.

Here sat two sisters blessed in so many ways except for the family genes that determined the route and result of everything we ate. We were beaten by our cravings. Sugar had won. Our resolve had collapsed.

"Tell no one," I said. "This is our secret."

We nodded to one another that we would not tell a living soul what we were about to do.

The next Saturday, I asked my mother if I could borrow her car to go to a movie with Linda. I had researched OA and found that meetings were held at a hospital thirty minutes from our home.

We easily found parking on the street. I turned off the engine. My sister and I took deep breaths and sat for a moment.

"Do you really think we should do this?" Linda asked looking at me, her older sister, for guidance.

"I don't know what else we can do," I answered gently. "I just don't think we have a choice anymore."

I felt so protective of my sister. What was I getting us into?

We opened our doors and both slowly got out of the car. We walked up the hospital sidewalk and entered through the door leading to the reception desk. We let others in line go ahead of us so no one would hear our question.

When we were alone at the reception desk, I put my face close to the receptionist's so she could hear me in my softest voice.

"Excuse me. Can you please tell us where Overeaters Anonymous meets?"

"Room 506," she answered. "Take the elevators behind you."

Linda swore that she then looked both of us up and down and smirked but I never saw it.

When the elevator opened on the fifth floor, Linda and I were frozen yet somehow disembarked. For ten minutes we tried to find room 506. The hospital layout was very confusing. When we finally found it, it did not look like an OA group meeting inside but rather a hospital staff meeting.

With shaky courage, I walked to the door and opened it. The entire room became silent and turned toward me.

In a whisper I asked the person sitting closest to the door, "Can you tell me where Overeaters Anonymous is meeting?"

And in the loudest volume a human is capable of producing, he answered, "OVEREATERS ANONYMOUS MEETS ACROSS THE HALL."

I told Linda I was sure that every staff member in that room looked me up and down and snickered.

Linda and I turned around and crossed the hall. We entered OA and sat down. It did not take five minutes to know we had made a huge mistake in coming there.

The members of this Chapter were hard core sugar addicts with life experience way beyond ours. If we were headed in that direction, we were nowhere close to being there yet. I took my sister's hand and we excused ourselves as being in the wrong place.

In the car, we looked at one another with relief.

"This may be the motivation we needed," Linda said. We drove to the movie theater and had no popcorn or candy.

THE RING

It was my sixteenth birthday. I slowly unwrapped the small box my parents had handed me. When I opened my gift, I was stunned to see the most beautiful ring I could have imagined. It was delicate and exquisitely designed with small pearls on either side and two small diamonds mounted around jade. It looked like a princess's crown. It was unique and I was thrilled. As I put it on my hand, I excitedly glanced up to show my parents and sisters how it looked. Suddenly, my sister Linda said "I wanted that ring. I saw it first." She burst out crying and left the room.

Linda was four years younger than I. It was a very painful moment for me when I realized that my sister had seen this ring in the store window and had wanted it. We both had fallen in love with the same piece of jewelry but it was now mine.

Linda and I had been close buddies when we were young but adolescence brought conflict between us and magnified our differences. It was not an easy time for us. Into adulthood, we remained loyal sisters and confidantes who saw almost everything in life as opposites. We were the sun and moon, never feeling or expressing the same emotions or opinions on almost anything except dancing and humor. But we always were devoted.

Linda was and always will be my favorite jitterbug partner. We light up the dance floor together and flow with our own grace, rhythm and joy.

When we are among people, if something happens or is said that is funny, our eyes meet across the room and we start to laugh. The more irreverent the humor, the harder we laugh. Sometimes we are the only two in hysterics at what we have seen or heard.

It was startling to me that my sister was about to celebrate her sixtieth birthday. This reality made me feel much older than sixty-four. How could Linda have already reached my decade? I had to make this milestone very special for her. She always said that I had gone through life's experiences first, marking a path for her and our sisters Susan and Ivy.

I gave her birthday celebration much thought. And then, in one moment, the inspiration came. It was clear to me how to honor this woman who had made me a sister.

I invited Linda to lunch on her birthday. After we ordered, I handed her a gift box. When she opened it, she just stared.

"It is now your turn," I said softly. "This ring that we both love has been mine for many years. It is now yours for the rest of your life."

Linda started to cry and said that she could not accept my magical ring.

"It is your turn," I repeated as I held her hand.

I hoped that through this gift my sister would understand how much I loved her. This ring was one of my most treasured possessions and now it would be hers.

From that day, Linda has never removed the ring from her finger. It looks so beautiful on her hand, and I am filled with profound joy knowing that we share a symbol of our life as sisters and that my gift has brought her such happiness.

THE DIVINE MISS M

Sitting and relaxing at a spa in California having just had a lemon peel facial, my eyes were closed when I heard that famous voice.

"You are glowing. Which facial did they give you?"

I opened my eyes and looked up at the smiling face of Bette Midler. She had just finished filming The Rose and was at La Costa Spa to unwind.

Later that afternoon we met again in the locker room.

"Would you like to go for a walk?" she asked.

Bette Midler was asking me if I would like to go for a walk. My knees almost buckled with excitement that I was trying to control and not show.

"I would love to," I answered.

As we walked and talked about oral interpretation of literature which we both studied and sisters whom we both loved and lost, I was touched by her sensitivity, charm and articulate manner. Her private persona was so different from her stage character. She was calm, soft spoken and empathic.

Being on the spa diet, I could only eat spa food. Therefore, when we stopped in a coffee shop because Bette was hungry and wanted to eat, I ordered only a diet coke. When customers approached our table for her autograph, she was most gracious.

Suddenly our waitress asked for my autograph.

"Why would you want my autograph?" I asked startled.

"I have never seen anyone from the spa come here and not break their diet," she answered smiling at me. I laughed.

Bette and I sat and talked, I realized that I would miss the spa dinner and have to go to bed on an empty stomach. I did not care. I would starve happily for this time with the Divine Miss M.

The next evening we met for drinks and talked more before I walked her to her limousine which would take her back to LA. We hugged good-bye and I watched her leave until I could no longer see her car. I always wondered why I did not ask her for her phone number or address. What I did have was an endearing memory of personal time spent with one of my favorite female entertainers. For a short while we were girlfriends. Our time together was divine.

WOULD YOU LIKE TO DANCE?

I am waiting for the boy to ask me to dance. My feelings are controlled and determined by junior high school aged boys. The best jitterbugger never asks me. My high school years will bring me popularity in dating older boys. But this is middle school years in the fifties and my pride is in the hands of boys who do the asking.

The most popular boy in school lives across the street. He is a basketball star although he has not yet grown into a man's height. He is the best dancer in my neighborhood group of friends. He always dances with the girls who will also kiss him. He knows how good-looking he is even at twelve. There is a line of females competing to dance with him, to be his girlfriend for a night, a week, a month. He is a sassy charmer. He knows he is number one.

I am not one of the girls who wants him but I like to watch the revolving door of his momentary picks. And what I really love is to watch him dance. He is a great dancer who has impeccable rhythm and knows all the latest steps. He is dazzling on the dance floor even in sixth, seventh and eighth grades.

One day I am twelve and the next I am sixty-three. The decades have brought me the marriage of my dreams, three incredible careers and a life in which I have been me. One of my greatest passions is dancing.

My childhood girlfriend is coming into town to attend the fiftieth anniversary of our high school. She talks me into going. I am not sure why she has to talk me into attending because I loved high school.

I was President of my Junior Class and spent four years being part of many activities. Although my junior high school classmates were there with me, interacting with new people was what I loved about high school.

I am not sure that this type of party, which is open to graduating classes spanning fifty years, will offer quality time to reminisce and visit. I receive some phone calls from old friends who have come to town. I decide to go.

It is a small group of my classmates who attend, maybe fifteen or so. Most of these classmates were with me in junior high as well as high school. I am thrilled to see them. One man walks up to me and says my name. I struggle to recognize his face. He then says his name and smiles. It is the star dancer of my adolescence, my former neighbor, the jock my pre-teen girlfriends lusted after.

We catch up on the moments that have brought us through six decades. As others arrive, I greet them and am greeted warmly. Everyone looks well. Sixty-three never looked better. These are the people of my youth. Their place in my life is a special one. The memories we share together are our beginning years.

The band is getting ready to play the oldies of the fifties and sixties. As the music begins, I walk toward the dance floor and turn. He catches my eye as I extend my hand toward him motioning for him to join me on the dance floor. The best jitterbugger in sixth grade takes my hand and we engage together in a graceful and wild ride singing the words to every song to which we are dancing. He is still a great dancer.

When our dance ends, I motion to another childhood male friend and then another. Each man joins me on the dance floor, one at a time. As boys, I had never danced with any of them. Now I am enjoying their individual style and movements. On that dance floor they are meeting me for the first time. And it is I who has asked them. I chose and picked the males with whom I wanted to dance that night.

One of my sisters is also there. When I talk to her at the end of the night, she tells me how wonderful I danced and how exciting it was that all the boys/men wanted to dance with me.

I smile to myself. I will always love the girl who was twelve and watched the dancers but a woman of sixty-three never felt better on the dance floor.

BACKSTAGE

I was in NYC and had spent another evening in the audience of a Broadway play. I had just seen Katharine Hepburn in Coco based on the life of Coco Chanel. The play was mediocre but I had come specifically to see Ms. Hepburn perform and she did not disappoint.

Leaving the theater, I noticed a large group of people were standing at the stage door. This was a tradition I had never taken part in but I found myself walking in their direction. Suddenly, the door opened a crack and a small group was ushered into the theater. I went in with them and was waiting for someone to turn around and ask "who are you?" To my great relief, it never happened.

First we were given a tour backstage. Then we walked through the theater itself and into the lobby where tables had been set up banquet style and a small orchestra was playing in one corner. This was a party being given for Ms. Hepburn who had just won the Oscar for the film The Lion in Winter.

I hung up my coat, had some delicious hors d'oeuvres and accepted an invitation to dance. As I left the dance area, I looked toward one corner of the room and saw Katharine Hepburn with her back to me speaking to some guests.

I walked over to her, waited until there was a break in her conversation and then tapped her on the shoulder. She turned around, looked at me and smiled. Her eyes were deep blue and her face had sculpted high cheek bones. She was breathtaking. Her tremor was obvious as it had been on stage.

"Ms. Hepburn, I have come in from Chicago to see you perform. I wish in my lifetime I might have known you as a friend."

Her eyes were locked into mine.

"You may have been disappointed, dear," she answered.

"I think not," I replied smiling.

With that last comment she nodded as though approving and turned back around to continue her conversation with her guests.

The stage had offered one part of the evening's performance. Backstage, I was magically transported into real life drama. I could not have had a more perfect and unexpected adventure.

Four

Home

RETRACING OLD STEPS

Seeing Chicago from your feet is really a perspective in experiencing your city that is unforgettably intimate. Going by bicycle, car, bus or roller blade will not do it in the same way. It has to be you, your feet and the city joined in a personal dance that allows you to feel the rhythms of Chicago's neighborhoods, lakefront and exquisite signature skyline.

Using the pedestrian walkway going north from Michigan Avenue onto the beach lakefront, while walking you can turn your head toward the skyline and watch it shine in the distance. After 9/11 each building became personal. Each represents the best of this city in its physical beauty, its diverse population and its historical architecture. We do not own these buildings but as Chicagoans they are ours.

As your feet move through the warm soothing sand, the sunlight orchestrates a free form ballet of glowing glass and steel. Chicago's skyline is the visible heartbeat of an exciting and proud American world-class city.

You turn your head to the right and there is blue. Blueness, blueosity, endless blue where the water meets the horizon. You climb down the levels of new fresh pavement to sit and dream. Your mind reaches out beyond what your eyes can see.

You continue your early morning walk through Chicago's Gold

Coast neighborhood. The shops are not yet open and the frenetic pace has not yet kicked in. For this moment it is only the sound of your feet on the pavement as you deliciously browse the windows in the various buildings that house an infinite variety of merchants making their livings in this urban setting. Cuisines, nails, massages, haircuts, coffee, banks, clothing. They are all there. With "closed" signs still on their doors, some are lit within beckoning with a promise of fulfillment to come. You stop and gaze. You feel the thriving pulse of city living. Your feet are engaged in a dance of their own as they carry you through the day's brisk yet quiet moments. You cannot get enough. You want this contemplation to last beyond the time all of this will belong to others as well.

Your steps continue down a familiar street. As you turn a corner, you find yourself standing in front of an apartment building in Lakeview. You look up at the top floor windows. Your husband has pointed out this location to you a million times. This is where he lived as a boy. This is where he strung tin cans to the apartment across the street where his friends who were twins lived. Young city boys talking to one another through their makeshift phone cans.

You try to imagine what it was like when your husband was a boy. You and he now live three blocks from this childhood site. You brought him back to the city because you would live nowhere else. He has given you an inch-by-inch tour of what the city neighborhood used to be like. Before the high rises on the lakefront were built there were vacant lots where he and his friends played. He remembers open spaces and high grass. He points out the restaurants that have survived as relics. He is especially proud of the piece of brick on his childhood apartment building where he carved his initials into fresh cement.

This visit has made you nostalgic for 4619, the address number of your old Albany Park neighborhood. The next weekend you find yourself standing in front of the door of your old apartment. To knock and walk in would change the reality of the memories you cherish. So you do not knock. You are not intrusive of the past. Instead you go for a walking tour of Albany Park that was once a gem. Your entire extended family lived in a two-block radius.

You know where you are headed. The candy store on the corner. As you approach you are shocked to see that it is still there. It is a basement shop. You slowly walk down the steps that were so steep for you as a child and enter. The memories of the smells and images of the penny candy and toys and coloring books and rainbow colored crayons are as real as they themselves had once been.

There is a woman behind the counter. You walk closer in disbelief. It is Mrs. S. She is still there. She looks up at you and after a long pause she says your name. She remembers. Her store represents some of the best memories of your youth in this city which you love so deeply. And she remembers you.

You continue five or six more blocks and there is your elementary school where your father had also attended as a boy. Architecturally, this is one of the old classic Chicago grammar schools. It is stately to the point of being intimidating. Or perhaps that is a perception of your youth.

You enter and walk the halls where you once waited for your milk and cookies. You walk into the auditorium where you left your mother's side for the first time when the kindergarten class lined up.

The school still stands and is functional. The neighborhood has changed cultures. Yet this could be one of many Chicago neighborhoods with its unforgettable legacy of community and tradition.

You continue walking. You pass one last shop. A shoe store. You make a mental note that you must return and reward your traveling companions.

HIS HOME

My husband Richard always says "our home" when he is telling about his wonderful life experiences. Half the time he is referring to the home he shared with his parents as an only child. His childhood was the stuff dreams are made of.

Richard's mother was a concert pianist. His parents came from Russia and kept that culture alive in their home through language, food and entertainment. Zina Joelson Aleskow was not only a gifted musician but also a wonderful cook of all the Russian foods my husband longs for to this day. Richard's father Gregory made his own Vodka. Guests begged him for the secret recipe which Richard has hidden away.

When world renowned musicians, conductors and composers came to Chicago to concertize, they would invariably come to the Aleskow home to play quartets, feast on excellent food and drink and enjoy the gracious hospitality that would inspire them to return time and time again.

As a young boy, Richard would sit on the couch in his feety pajamas taking in an adult world. He loved being around these artistic, creative and accomplished musicians. His home was always filled with guests and their music. Most importantly, his ears were filled with the beauty of his mother's piano as she played for hours either rehearsing or entertaining. His was a classical music home where he developed a lifelong passion for this genre.

Years after his father died, his mother lived alone in her apartment continuing to play, having guest quartets in her home and giving dinner parties. When his mother was in her nineties, Richard asked her if she would like to move to a senior home. In reply she asked him "why would I want to be around old people?"

When his mother was ninety-three, her youngest sister was to celebrate her eightieth birthday. Richard's aunts lived in Duluth, Minnesota. That meant my mother-in-law would have to fly from Chicago. She was hesitant but Richard convinced her to go with us. Richard also called his cousins around the country and told them to come to the party and surprise their aunts. It was a wondrous weekend celebration. Every time a nephew or niece entered the house, the aunts screamed with joy. Richard's mom thanked him and told him it was the best weekend she had ever had.

Richard and I returned to Chicago before my mother-in-law. She flew back with Richard's first cousin and his wife. When we called her, she did not answer her phone. Richard told me not to worry because she liked to wash her hair late at night. When she still did not answer by midnight, Richard and I got dressed and ran the few blocks from our apartment to hers.

When Richard opened her door with the key he had to her apartment, we saw her sitting at her dining room table in her robe with her mail spread out in front of her. Richard called "Mom". She looked like she had fallen asleep. Richard walked up to her and felt her pulse.

"She is gone."

"What are you saying?" I answered.

"She is gone," my husband repeated.

We stood there looking at one another through our tears. I called 911 and Richard went downstairs to the building's lobby to wait for them.

It was as though my mother-in-law's life had been tied in a bow and she had been kissed goodnight. She died peacefully in the home she loved surrounded by her piano, her favorite pieces of furniture, her cherished music library and the memories that would live on through her son.

MR. X & MR. Y

It often happens like that. Strangers regularly meet in the same place by coincidence or necessity and share discourse on some level. It might be small talk or profound thoughts. It might be politics or current events. It might be shoptalk or gossip. The one constant is that the strangers do not exchange names.

So it was for these two men. Both were lawyers. Both lived their devotion to the American dream. Every few weeks they met in the hallway of the courthouse. They shared discussions of their upcoming cases. Both were defense attorneys. One was devoted to helping the underprivileged. He was a private attorney who would take a case whether his client could pay him or not. The other often helped his countrymen who like himself had come to the United States to make their home.

These two men were old-fashioned gentlemen. They were from the old school of manners and dedication. They loved the law and this country. They loved helping people. In time they related like old friends.

Mr. X was a Russian immigrant who came to the United States when he was in his teens. He put himself through college and law school and created his legal practice. Word spread throughout the community that he was a caring and empathic lawyer. He had a wife who was a concert pianist and a son who was the gift of his life. He and his wife called their son their dividend.

Mr. Y was married with two sons. He was born to practice law.

He was a man who loved to talk and who believed in the essence of American justice and fairness. He was exemplary in his legal work. He was a champion of the poor.

Mr. Y was attracted to Mr. X's style and demeanor. Mr. X wore pince-nez glasses. He was dignified with an old world charm and grace. Mr. Y loved their talks as they waited to appear in court. They had become two friendly strangers who knew nothing of one another but the fact that they were both attorneys in America's courtrooms.

Years later Mr. X died. Mr. Y looked for his friend but finally realized something must have happened to him.

One night Mr. Y who was my Uncle Sam Linn was invited to my fiancé's mother's home for dinner to celebrate our engagement. As my Uncle walked into my future mother-in-law's dining room, he looked at a large oil portrait hanging on the wall. He stared at the painting almost unable to speak.

"Is this your husband?" he asked stunned.

My fiancé answered first. "Yes, that is my father Gregory Aleskow."

"I knew him from court," my Uncle responded. "He was an elegant man. We used to talk all the time in the courthouse hallway. I liked him so very much."

We all stood looking at the portrait of my future husband Richard's father.

"I cannot believe this," my Uncle said softly almost speaking to himself.

"I knew him and loved talking to him."

We celebrated two occasions that night. We made a special toast to the reunion of two friends and colleagues who shared a mutual admiration for each other and this country and were about to become relatives through marriage.

HER CHILDHOOD POSSE

One Chanukah my grandfather gave all his granddaughters dolls and all his grandsons and me a toy gun. Times have changed. I am not thrilled with a society of guns as an adult, but being a tomboy, my entire childhood was consumed with my fantasy of being a cowboy. When not in school, I was always dressed in my Western finest. If I was not in my Western pants, a cowgirl skirt was acceptable as long as I was wearing my gear. My cowboy hat never left my head even during Chicago's hottest summer days.

My friend Steve and his brother Bobby along with my sister Linda were my neighborhood playmates. We always played cowboys and Indians and I always made the rules of our imaginary West. My younger sister Linda was always killed off as the Indian and went crying to my mother that I and my posse of boys had ridden off leaving her nothing to do.

I would spend hours detailing every aspect of what everyone's horses looked like. This all came from my imagination but it was as real to me as a living, galloping horse would be. Describing my horse was my childhood at its happiest. I rode a Palomino. As my posse sat glued to my every word, I gave an inch by inch portrait of the stately and breathtaking horse I proudly rode around the neighborhood. We cared for our horses and groomed them. The level of pantomime in which we engaged was inspirational childhood creativity. Yet, it was reality to me. My backyard and the sidewalks around my house were the brush and boulders of the Western lands I had seen in my favorite cowboy television series and movies.

The Lone Ranger was my idol. Silver took my breath away. My favorite sound was the clip clop of horses' hooves as they carried their loyal cowboys throughout western towns and prairies. The friendship between my cowboy heroes and their horses touched me deeply. They continually saved one another.

There were some shocking realities that interrupted my perfect fantasy of life in the West. I remember watching an episode of The Cisco Kid in which the bad guy purposely had to keep his hand on his gun in his holster while waiting to draw against Cisco because The Kid's gun got stuck in his holster. I was appalled at how phony that moment was. I immediately lost all respect for Cisco. I knew that even I could have outdrawn him.

As much as I loved school, I could not wait to come home every day to play cowboys and Indians. Poor Linda has never forgotten her sad role in my Western stories and plots. And then one day we added another member to our posse.

It was a hot summer afternoon. My cousins Eddie and Larry were visiting. Being the tomboy that I was, that was always a special treat. My father had just brought home a German Shepherd puppy that morning. I picked up the new puppy and we all headed to our backyard to play Rin Tin Tin. We were utterly amazed at how quickly Dream Girl became one of us. Every time we shot Linda and she fell to the ground, our genius puppy would go to her and put her paw on the body.

We were playing for an hour or so when Dream Girl collapsed. We all ran to her standing over her in a circle. She did not move. I ran into the apartment yelling for my father to come. "The puppy is dead," I screamed. He ran out to the yard and informed us that playing in the hot sun, the puppy had fainted. She needed shade and water. "Remember," he cautioned, "she is just a baby."

I was more careful with my new dog whose papers indicated that she was the great granddaughter of Rin Tin Tin the third. She became an integral part of our posse and my inspired cowboy games.

To this day my toy cowboy gear that my grandfather gave to me is among my favorite childhood possessions. Looking at it brings back so many memories of the splendorous games of my cowboy past. I could not be prouder or happier to have been a part of the Wild West without having left the Midwest.

DREAM GIRL

My sisters and I stood at the living room window and watched my father get out of the car. He was holding a brown cardboard box. In anticipation, my two year old sister Susan took one look at the box and promptly threw up. So began her childhood fear of dogs.

My dad entered the apartment holding the box. He lowered it so I could see what was inside and that was the first moment I saw our new German Shepherd, Dream Girl.

It was a hot summer afternoon. My cousins Eddie and Larry were visiting. Being the tomboy that I was, seeing them was always a special treat. However, my sister, Linda, always complained that during our games of cowboys and Indians she was the first to get killed off.

I picked up the new puppy and we headed to our backyard to play Rin Tin Tin. We were utterly amazed at how quickly Dream Girl became one of us. Every time we shot Linda and she fell to the ground, our genius puppy would go to her and put a paw on the body.

We were playing for an hour or so when Dream Girl collapsed. We all ran and stood over her in a circle. She did not move. I ran into the apartment yelling for my father to come.

"The puppy is dead," I screamed.

He hurried to the yard and informed us that playing in the hot sun, the puppy had fainted. She needed shade and water.

"Remember," he cautioned, "she is just a baby."

Although Linda and I were very comfortable with this quickly growing puppy, my sister Susan kept her distance and was increasingly afraid. We had a knotty-pine den in the apartment with a full door that could be used as a half door. One could close the bottom half and leave the upper half open. Very early one morning while my parents and I were asleep, Linda was in the den playing with Dream Girl. Susan watched from what she considered the safe side of the half-open door.

Stroking Dream Girl, Linda taunted Susan. "I dare you to come in here and pet this dog. I know you are a scared baby and will never come close to the dog," she continued on her mission.

"I am not a baby," Susan cried.

"Then prove it," Linda, the young psychologist countered.

Sure enough when my parents and I woke, there was my sister Susan proudly petting the gentle Shepherd. Linda stood next to them both with a smile of triumph. It was the end of Susan's fear of dogs.

I loved Dream Girl with all my heart. My family moved to a house within the next year. Most unfortunately, my mother was not a dog lover. With our new white carpet, Dream Girl was only allowed in certain rooms of the house.

One afternoon while my mother was out shopping, Dream Girl and I had the run of the house. Unfortunately, I did not hear my mom's car pull into the driveway in time to bring Dream Girl downstairs. When my mom entered the house, Dream Girl and I were playing in the white carpeted living room. My mom started yelling at me to get the dog out of there. Dream Girl, startled and frightened, began urinating on my mother's new carpeting. The more my mother yelled, the more my dog urinated while running in circles around the room as I tried to catch her. Both Dream Girl and I were in the dog house over that episode.

One night there was a terrible rainstorm. The lightening was blinding and the thunder was deafening. As I walked down the stairs toward the garage, I saw water seeping in under the door. My first thought was of Dream Girl; she was out in the garage. As I opened the door my mother was yelling, "Do not open that door."

The flooded garage water knocked me over as it entered the house. Swimming on top of it was my precious dog. She swam to me and started licking me as I sat soaked on the floor. I held her tight and kissed her back.

My mother was so distracted by the flood she did not even notice that my German Shepherd and I headed upstairs to my bedroom. I took a towel and tenderly dried her. That night she slept with me in my bedroom.

My dad had a German Shepherd when he was a boy. He loved them. His dog appeared on his doorstep one night during a storm so he called him Stormy. This dog became my father's personal protector. One day a buddy of Dad's came up behind him and playfully put a chokehold on him. Stormy plunged toward the boy and if my dad had not caught the leash, the dog would have attacked. Dad was always convinced that Stormy was a lost military dog. Then one day, as he came, so he left.

When my father bought Dream Girl, her papers stated she was the great, great granddaughter of Rin Tin Tin the third. I was very proud of this pedigree. Even so, my dad claimed she was not as smart as his dog because he had trouble house breaking her. I, on the other hand, thought she was not only smart but as loving and attentive as one could hope for in any sensitive friend. Her name fit her well. And, although she belonged to the family, there was no doubt in my mind that she was my dog.

As life would have it, I dearly love dogs but Dream Girl has been my only dog. As an adult, my husband and I live in a condo building that does not allow animals but has the most beautiful views of Chicago imaginable. It is a hard choice to have made to stay here because I desperately want a dog but the view is a treasure.

I live along the lake where there is a dog beach I visit often. I am the only one there without a dog. Whenever I see a German Shepherd, I stop and lovingly stroke the memory of my Dream Girl.

THE ELEVATOR

It started as any other workday. Around 7:15 a.m. I gathered my purse, briefcase and water bottle, locked the door of my apartment on the thirty-fifth floor of my Chicago high-rise and walked toward my building's four elevators, one of which would take me to the first floor garage and my car.

Elevator #1 stopped on thirty-five and its doors opened. I stepped inside as I had done every weekday morning for years. I was the only one in the elevator. At floor twenty-one the elevator stopped, its doors opened and a woman got in. We smiled at each other with that morning look that expressed hope our remaining ride down would be an express to the ground floor.

We both stood facing the elevator door staring at the floor numbers lighting up one at a time. When the elevator approached the seventeenth floor, it abruptly stopped. All the lights on its panel went out. For a second we both stood silently trying to assess what had happened. Then I heard the sounds of my neighbor starting to hyperventilate. I quickly told her it would be OK. I calmly reached over to the panel on the wall and pushed the door open button. Nothing. I pushed it again. Nothing.

Now she started to panic. I knew that it would not take much more for me to also lose it so I focused on calming her. I pushed the alarm and then the telephone button. The connection was directly to the alarm company. I informed them that two women were stuck in an elevator, what seemed now a rather small elevator, and gave them the address of our building. I asked if the operator could connect me with the security guard in my building.

I remember thinking that it made no sense to me that I could not directly call my building from the elevator phone. My neighbor and I both tried our cell phones but they were dead. Suddenly, the voice of our building's security was on the phone. He told us that the maintenance staff had been looking for us because they could not identify what floor we were on. I knew that the building's manager came to work every day at 6 am so I asked that they notify her.

After the security guard disconnected, the other woman looked at me and for a moment we were both frozen. Here we were, two strangers living anyone's and everyone's nightmare. One of us had claustrophobia and the other had a potential for it in this situation. It was at that moment that I am certain we both privately made the decision to help the other by not falling apart. This was fortunate because we were about to spend two and one half hours trapped inside that elevator.

After about five more minutes, which seemed like infinity, I again pushed the phone button and asked the operator if a service person was on the way. She answered honestly that they were trying to get in touch with him. We were in the city and he lived in a distant suburb. My partner and I started yelling at the operator, demanding that they contact a service provider who lived closer. She answered that they did not have one. It was incredulous.

I tried to control my anger aware that this operator was all we had. She was our link to the outside world. She was very empathic and apologetic. We had to keep her that way.

Then suddenly we heard banging on the outside elevator door. It was the building manager. My new acquaintance and I looked at each other. We started yelling for help. The manager yelled back that because of a new city ordinance she could not try to get the door open until the elevator repairperson arrived.

We begged her. She stood her ground although most apologetically. She told us that there was a water main that had flooded near the expressway exit and our repairperson was stuck in the traffic jam around it. She tried to engage us in conversation. She assured us that the elevator would not fall. Until she mentioned it, that thought had never occurred to me.

My cellmate and I together faced something worse than potential danger. We faced the agony of irrational fear and panic. We had to make a choice. It was then that the humanity happened. We started telling each other our life's stories. We took turns. We smiled and laughed. Then suddenly one of us would remember where we were and that we were trapped. We could see it in each other's eyes when it happened. One of us would drift away and go inside where a consuming terror threatened rationality and focus.

At that moment, the other would work harder to entertain and engage. We were relating like old friends who moved together gracefully with purpose. We were at that time and in that space devoted strangers who had bonded.

The first elevator repairperson finally made it. He, however, could not figure out the problem so he called for assistance. We pleaded for them to just pull the doors open. We had both seen this done a million times in movies. They were sorry but they could not. The approach to freedom had to begin on top of the elevator car.

In our cramped quarters, my new companion and I paced and talked. We knew somehow that each was keeping the other from absolutely losing it. She was my lifeline and I was hers. Logically one knows how it will end. However, not being able to leave a space can paralyze one with desperation.

When the doors were finally pried open, we were between floors. I let her go first. When I was helped out, she and I embraced and cried. It was the first tears we had shed that day. There had been no room in that elevator for tears. There had only been space for two strangers and their caring for one other.

We have seen each other in the building now and then. We are usually rushing in or out with bags and packages. We always pause and smile. We remember the terror. We acknowledge the miraculous connection that happened between us.

Five
The Professor

THE HAT

It started as a typical first class session of the new semester at Wright College in Chicago. Twenty-five faces were staring at me with the fear of college students who would prefer to be anywhere in the world other than a communication class. As I looked back at them with all the empathy I could express, I asked that everyone wearing hats please remove them. They looked at me with that confusion of a generation unfamiliar with such etiquette.

The hats were removed except for one young man's. When I asked him directly, he answered "no." I was shocked but did not show it. Not ten minutes into the session and in front of new students whom I was meeting for the first time, I was being challenged. How I handled this moment could determine semester survival. My semester survival.

The students were intently watching me and waiting. It was my move. I decided not to deal publicly with this challenge to my authority so I asked to see the young man after class. His name was Mark and he looked like the most unlikely of all the students to express insubordination. He was slight in build, clean cut with a pleasant face. He was not someone who stood out among the others. Yet he had said "no" to a directive from his new professor in front of new classmates on the first day of the new semester. There would be no choice. I had to convince him to do what the others were asked. He would have to back down.

After class, alone in my classroom, Mark and I faced one another. His eyes focused toward the floor. He would not look at me as I spoke. His hat, the symbol of his defiance, still sat securely on his head.

"Mark," I said softly, "you must follow the rules of this class. Removing your hat demonstrates respect. Is there a reason you feel you must wear your hat? I am willing to listen."

Mark lifted his eyes and looked into mine. "No," he answered. His look was empty. His tone was flat.

"Then you must remove it," I answered in my most professorial voice. He did as I asked.

At that moment I recognized my challenge with this young man. He complied in removing his hat but I had not reached him. I had forced him but I had not persuaded him.

Slowly throughout the semester, I felt a bond growing between Mark and me. Sometimes he would even smile at my jokes and ask thoughtful questions in class. When I saw him in the hall, he would tip his hat. I would not let him see me smile at that obvious gesture.

The final week of the semester Mark asked me to stay after class. He had something to tell me which he had kept secret.

I had come to know him as a gifted poet and hardworking writer and speaker. Harder than most perhaps because Mark suffered from MS which had affected his coordination and vocal cords. Some days the class and I understood him better than others.

"Do you remember the first day of class when I refused to remove my hat?" he asked.

"Oh yes I do," I answered.

"Well, now I would like to tell you why I did that. About a year ago I went to an open mic forum to read my poetry. They laughed at me."

"They what?" I asked not wanting to believe what I was hearing.

"They laughed."

His speech was labored and painfully slow. "I was humiliated."

Once again like that first day of class we were alone in my classroom. We looked at one another through our tears.

"The first day of this class when I refused to remove my hat I was trying to get you to throw me out of your class. The course was required but I did not want to ever stand before an audience again and perform my writing. But you would not give up on me. You would not let me leave."

"You chose to stay, Mark," I answered softly. We stood there for a moment looking at one another.

For his final persuasive speech, Mark spoke on Stem Cell Research Funding. He passionately argued for our government to acknowledge that it is his quality of life they are ignoring and for his classmates to vote for legislators who would make the stem cell reality happen. Would it be soon enough for him we all agonizingly wondered?

After offering an articulate and informed argument, with great difficulty Mark walked to his visual aid which was an empty white poster board. He asked his audience to give him one thing. Only one thing. He picked up a marker and with a shaking hand one letter painstakingly at a time he wrote, "Hope."

A year after he had completed my course, Mark came to my office to say hello. He proudly told me that students from our class would stop him in the hall and tell him that they would never forget his last speech. The MS was progressive and he was suffering. Yet he looked happy and at peace with himself. He had formed a team in his name for the MS Walk each year and was trying to raise money to help himself and others through funding for research.

Three years later I received an e-mail from him. He wanted me to know that he was writing again and that for the first time since he had been traumatized by the experience he again performed his poetry in an open mic at a Chicago club. He said he could have never done it without my course and my friendship. In his last line he told me that he always wore his cherished hat.

MY OFFICE

In January 1994, I left the role of General Manager of WYCC-TV, a PBS affiliate in Chicago, and joined the faculty of Wright College as Assistant Professor of Communication. I was forty-nine years old and changing careers. As always I had my husband's invaluable support.

The Chairperson of the Speech Department of which I was now a member gave me the choice of two offices from which to choose. The end office was smaller than the others. It had a slanted wall that reminded me of Emily Dickinson's attic in which she would write and create her works. That thought sold me on Office L331 which became my professional home.

The first thing I did was to hang my television and community service plaques and awards. Next I positioned the picture of my staff at the station that had been given to me as a gift. I put my teaching supplies in my desk drawer. School supplies! Whether as a student or a teacher they thrilled me. They were my earliest memories of school, of the beginning of each semester, of newness and anticipation. They were treasures. One of my colleagues stopped by to welcome me. "I see you have already nested," she said smiling.

I looked at the remaining spaces on the walls of my new office. I was returning to the classroom after being away for many years. Did I still have the ability to connect with students the way I had always done? Could I still create the magic I had experienced in the classroom? Would I ever receive anything from my future students or from my academic work that I could proudly hang in those spaces?

January 2007. I am a Full Professor. I have been named the 2007 Distinguished Service Professor of Wright College. My office walls are filled with academic awards and honors, certificates of acknowledgement and gifts from my students.

Yet the memories that I cherish most in this Emily Dickinson-like attic room are those that cannot be seen. The faces of the students who have visited me, the stories that students have shared with me, the work students have shown me. In my thirteen years at Wright, I have taught hundreds of students. I have a deep respect for the community college student who does it all at once. School, work, family, all at the same time.

Some of the stories I have heard in this office are unforgettable. The young man with MS who struggled to overcome his fear of performance and his inability to speak clearly due to his illness. The English as a Second Language students who came to a new country, a new city and struggled to do Public Speaking in English, a foreign language to them. The single mothers and fathers who were trying desperately to arrange for affordable child care so that they could attend class. The endless stories of grandmothers who died each time an assignment was due or an exam missed. The student who looked and sounded exactly like Travolta's character Tony in *Saturday Night Fever* and who told me that he was in college on a bet. The female students who were in doomed marriages and who were seeking another way to live their lives and to support themselves. The Muslim student who was afraid for her own personal safety after September 11th. The Caucasian male who could not understand why the family of his Hispanic girlfriend would not accept him. The student who cut herself whenever she faced pressure. Student after student afraid to speak before an audience. Students who were lonely. Students who ended relationships. Students who came back to tell me that they had completed Medical School, Law School, Graduate School. Students who got the job they wanted, the promotion they hoped for, the first apartment of their own.

I sit in my office, in the privacy of this cherished space remembering. I remember their voices, their smiles, their tears. They have been not only my work but also my family. To them I am devoted. My walls tell the story of my career. My heart holds the meaning of my career. The family of students whom I have taught will always belong to me and I to them.

Six

Friends and Strangers

THERE FOREVER

We had long talks while sharing a paddle boat on the lake near both our apartments in Chicago's Lincoln Park. My friend was decades older than I which gifted me her wisdom and extraordinary insights and perceptions. Our talks in that boat taught me life lessons I will carry with me until the day I die.

One Sunday as we drifted on the pond talking and enjoying each other's thoughts, my friend suddenly said: "When I die, I hope to come back as a seagull."

"Why a seagull?" I asked.

I smiled as I watched my dear friend staring at the seagulls flying over the glistening water.

"They are graceful and free. That is my hope."

It was very painful for me when my friend retired and moved to another state. Visiting her was not the same as sharing time with her on a regular basis in Chicago. We had to rely on the phone and e-mails to stay in touch. Our connection and understanding of one another were so strong that our discussions never lost their depth or truth.

I will never forget the e-mail I opened that day:

And now the truth about me and all. I have lung cancer. Termination date two months. I am writing this because I cannot talk very well and get so breathless. I have hospice coming the last week and they have been superb. As of yesterday I took to bed because I am so weak. Other than weakness, I have no pain. Since January I have suspected that something was wrong. I am relieved to know the truth. I am ready in all ways to join my energy with outer space. The body has become rusty--- eyes, ears, joints and lungs. It is my time and I am completely at one with nature. So be with me and experience the relief from all troubles I have. I will always be with you in spirit. Love to you always. Your devoted friend.

I was stunned. I started to cry and could not stop.

She was able to send me more e-mails during the time she was dying. I cherished every word she used her strength to share and always replied with the gratitude that my beloved friend was still able to receive my notes. I was even able to briefly speak to her by phone although her energy was almost gone.

And then the last e-mail came:

This may be the last letter I can send. I am not supposed to exert too much energy. I have no pain but no appetite, no energy, and sleep most of the time. The end will come soon--- I hope. I know that this is a difficult time for you, and my heart goes out to you. The spirit is a strong bond and will be there forever. Love always.

Over and over I re-read the last e-mails and all the cards and notes I had received from her over the years of our friendship. Her written words were priceless and helped me to feel close to her.

Several weeks after my friend died, I took a walk along the lake where we had always gone to talk. I was profoundly sad and longed to speak with her. As I stood lost in my thoughts while looking at the water, I suddenly felt a presence near me. I slowly turned my head and looked down. There next to me was a beautiful seagull. It was looking up at me. Neither of us moved for quite a while. I felt a calm within me. Then, I smiled, and the seagull flew away to freedom.

WAITING

My beloved girlfriend,

Who else can really understand how much we love each other? You are so sick as I write this and I am so far away. Your family has kept me updated and I am deeply grateful to them. But this is so hard. You are in such danger and there is nothing I can do but pray for you. We are all praying for you.

It happened within hours. You were rushed to the hospital Saturday morning with acute pancreatitis. The doctors are not sure why this has happened. All the side effects one can develop have happened. You could not breathe and were intubated. The situation is dire. It is life threatening. I am devastated and terrified.

Oh Ar, I miss you so. I miss talking to you through our e-mails and phone calls and getting your detailed updates of happenings.

I am thinking back to that first moment we met. I had transferred to a new junior high and was sitting in the lunch room with a girl whom I had met in one of my classes. There was only one other person at this new school whom I knew although not well. His name was Jeff and he had gone to my other school before his family moved to the same neighborhood where my family and I now lived.

As my acquaintance and I were having lunch, I looked across the lunch room and saw a group of girls marching toward me from the opposite end of the huge room. They were in single file walking behind a girl who looked like their leader. She was pretty with her hair pulled back in a ponytail. That was the first time I saw you.

When you reached my table, you bent toward me, looked me in the eye and said: "Jeff is *my* boyfriend!"

Then you turned on your heel and every girl in that line turned in unison with you and you all walked away. You reminded me of the synchronized Rockettes.

I asked the girl sitting with me, "who was that?"

"The popular girls," she sniffed.

I sat at the table stunned. Jeff had never been my boyfriend. Your warning was loud and clear but misplaced.

I know you don't like it when I tell this story of how we met because by the summer we had become best friends and you prefer not to remember our initial so-called introduction.

We have been dearest friends since we were nine. We have just celebrated receiving Medicare. We have shared a lifetime of laughter and devastation.

I remember our sleepovers when you introduced me to your favorite late night snack of crackers soaked in milk. And you had to wait until I woke in the morning because you were an early riser and I loved to sleep late.

We will never forget our joint assignment from the high school newspaper. Feeling very adult, we traveled to downtown Chicago to interview Sandra Dee. It was a press conference for high school reporters. Sandra Dee was at the height of her popularity as an actress.

You inched your way through the crowd to stand behind her to see if you could spot any dark roots in her blonde hair. Later, you and I talked on the phone half the night planning how we might contact her to offer to be her best friends because we felt that she seemed lonely.

We doubled in high school dating best male friends. We were quite a foursome. And throughout junior high and high school, you always remained the dazzling leader of the pack. Although I spread my wings to other friends and new people, you and I always stayed close.

It is not only the memories but the nuances of our lives that we cherish together.

You and I were cleaning out the garage at my house when we were thirteen and my mom left for the hospital to give birth to my third sister Ivy. And I have been your confidant as you have struggled bravely after the death of your husband.

You are my special friend, my lifelong friend. You are and always have been sunshine.

You are the history of my life. You are my only friend who calls me by my family nickname. You are the friend who has purchased every magazine and anthology my work is in and who celebrates my publishing successes as though they are your own.

You are still in the hospital's ICU. I cannot talk with you. I hold on tightly to the sound of your voice in my head.

I am waiting for you, my girlfriend... I am waiting.

God be with you and make you well.

All my love always.

Your girlfriend,

Elynne

PostScript: I did get to hear her voice again and speak to her every day until the end.

December 24, 1944 -- March 14, 2011

Arlene Orlove Ray was one of the most beautiful, kind, loyal and perceptive human beings to have graced this world. The devastation of her loss is immeasurable. I am numb. I cannot imagine a world without my lifelong friend.

THE SHADOW

I was in my own thoughts as I drove down one of Chicago's main boulevards on my way to grocery shopping. The traffic was heavy as usual on this street of two-flat apartment buildings so I was traveling very slowly. My favorite radio station kept me relaxed.

Suddenly through my peripheral vision, I sensed motion on the sidewalk to my left. The traffic was temporarily stopped as I turned my head. A young woman was running out of one of the two-flat buildings. She looked panicked. She was barefoot. She ran from the building into the street and up to my car window where she started pounding and yelling for me to open the door. She kept looking back at the building with terror in her eyes.

It was a split second gut affirming decision to unlock my car door and allow this stranger in. I knew she was in trouble and I knew she needed my help. The immediacy of her desperation scared me for both of us. Was someone about to appear from that building with a gun aimed at her and me? At the very moment of that thought, the traffic started to move and she and I left the scene of her escape.

It was her husband. He beat her often. She needed to get out but had been afraid to leave him. She thought that this time he would have killed her.

"Will you please take me to my mother's house?" she pleaded.

"Of course," I answered without having a clue where I was being asked to drive.

On the way to her mother's, which was approximately a thirty minute drive, we talked and kept watching the cars behind us in case he had followed.

"You showed courage," I told her. "Perhaps you are ready to take back your self-esteem and your life."

She listened intently to my words and encouragement. She was just beginning to think of the possibilities of her life free from abuse. She had difficult decisions to make and yet, she knew that the bottom line was her survival and quality of life. Even without any other plans or answers at this time, I could feel she knew that.

When we pulled up to her mother's house, she turned to me in silence and looked at me for what seemed like a long time. Then she took my hand and squeezed it.

"You can do this," I whispered.

She opened the car door and was gone.

LIFE 101

I will never forget taking the constitution test in junior high. My classmates and I were so nervous. Even though I got good grades in school, I was always sure I failed after taking a test. I was a good student but I was a better worrier. In worrying I excelled.

This was the morning we would learn if we passed the exam. Nervously we entered Mr. B's class. He had draped the board in black. The list was posted. My heart was in my throat as I walked toward the board. There was my name under the word *failed.* I froze. As I tried to hold them back, tears filled my eyes. I was devastated as I returned to my desk.

Mr. B was watching me for what seemed a very long time. Suddenly he burst out laughing. He walked up to the board, tore down the list and put up a second list, the real list that showed that I and many others had passed. A wonderful joke he thought.

Years later I became a college professor. Mr. B had taught me a lesson I would never forget. From my years as a student and a Professor, I offer my communication life survival skills insights.

- I know a place
- It is private
- It can take you anywhere you want to go
- It can be with you so you are not alone

- It can lead you through your fears to where you feel safe
- It can give you courage
- It can help you to dream and make you determined
- This place is yours. It belongs only to you.

THIS PLACE IS YOUR MIND

USE IT WELL!

Use it to celebrate your gender.
Do not use your gender to abuse others!

Use it to respect the foundation of your race,
ethnicity and religion.
Do not limit your life by them.

Use it to build your self-esteem---- how you
feel about yourself.
Do not sell your self-esteem, or bargain for
it, or give it away for any reason.

Some people have a hole in their self-esteem...
*H*ole

To make that hole into a complete self---
a whole you.... *W*hole

The difference is a **W**

- You need **W**ill
- You need **W**ant

- You need **Work**
- You need **We**

Your **WILL** is your determination and focus
to reach your potential
to be the best **YOU** that you can be and
to make your dreams happen.

YOU can make your dreams happen.

WANT is your desire to care about yourself—
your dignity, your hopes, your
accomplishments, your pride!

WORK is the effort it takes and the planning
required to do well.

WE are the relationships to which you devote
yourself.

Pick your friends carefully. Surround yourself with others who bring out the best in you.

Remember that a whole life--- **Whole**----
Begins with me but focuses on we.

Through the process of building a strong self-esteem, you will become independent. You will face your fears and walk through them coming out the other side.

Do not waste your time worrying over what is past. As you go through life, you will experience happiness and pain, milestones and transitions. No matter what happens remember one thing. You will never be alone. You have your self-esteem. ***You have you.***

STRANGERS ON THE STEPS

I was so concerned about how we would get our bags on the train that even though I spoke basic French, I had our Paris hotel staff translate to French: *We are in need of help to put our luggage on the train.* For the first time in our lives, my husband and I felt like seniors. Ok, young seniors. Together we were traveling throughout Europe by train. Although we were not yet ready for Tauck Tours, negotiating our luggage on and off trains was difficult.

The day started with our Paris Hotel not giving us our wake-up call. I should have known this was an omen. Luckily, I did not sleep well and was up at 6am to wake Richard who sleeps worry free.

We were picked up by our driver early with plenty of time to get to the train station so I could find assistance for our bags. When we reached the train station for the Chunnel, which was to be the experience of a dream come true for Richard, our driver commented on a strange event happening within the station, abruptly wished us bonne chance, and left us.

There was a line of over seven hundred people wrapped around the inside of the station. The elevators and escalators had been turned off. People had missed their trains because the trains too had been stopped. The Chunnel had been closed because of a bomb scare and resulting security problems.

When security finally allowed people to proceed, they had to carry their luggage up over one hundred nonmoving escalator stairs. There was no way Richard could get our luggage up those stairs. I frantically went to the ticket window and handed them my handwritten hotel note in its perfect French. Yet, the response was that there was no one to help us.

If we were going to leave Paris by Chunnel with our luggage, we would have to find a miracle. Suddenly and unasked, other passengers saved us by pulling and carrying part of our cases while Richard and I pulled the others. A young woman selflessly helped Richard while the man behind me on the escalator grabbed my suitcase with one hand and carried it to the top. I hugged him so tightly that he looked in shock at my gesture of gratitude.

At the top, the young woman smiled and asked me "Don't you believe in angels?"

A traveling nightmare became a moment where the kindness of strangers defined our vacation.

LUCY

Having raised her children, divorced, and now enjoying the devotion of young grandchildren, one of my dearest girlfriends decided it was her time to enjoy her second chapter. She quickly mastered the challenges of on-line dating.

Lucy is a very attractive woman with intelligence and a wonderful sense of humor. Males are attracted to her. Her mystique seems to mesmerize them. So many of the men she has met on-line have fallen hard for her. Her scenario would be most women's dream, but Lucy is specific about her choices and after seeing a man a few times, she often becomes disillusioned.

As her happily married confidant, it has been my role to listen and advise. Many men have hoped she was the one, but she and I have spent hours thinking up ways to let them down gently.

"Tell him it is you and has nothing to do with him."

"Tell him you have gone back with your old boyfriend."

This last excuse always brought the same response to me from Lucy.

"If I tell him I am back with my old boyfriend, he will see I am still on the on-line dating service. I can't say that."

We would try to think up excuse after excuse. It was hard for Lucy to disappoint a suitor with one of our excuses, but she did so over and over. After she would finally find the courage to make her speech, she would then question whether she had made the right decision in letting them go. It was my memory she relied on.

"Do you remember the sound of his voice drove you crazy? Do you remember he was cheap? Do you remember you had nothing in common?"

Getting accustomed to the new rules of second chapter dating was not easy. Lucy tried to explain it to me.

"One is never invited for dinner initially. It is coffee or a drink."

"Even at dinner time?" I would ask. "I know you are hungry. Isn't he?"

"Sometimes if I pass the test, drinks go into dinner but not necessarily," Lucy explained. "Dinner may have to be a second date."

I always shook my head when I heard this. These were established men not twenty-year-olds. Certainly they could afford to buy a woman dinner.

One morning Lucy called me laughing. "This you will not believe," she said.

She had told me that the norm was for people to lower their age on their on-line profile. For some reason, she had decided to tell a new caller that there had been a computer glitch and that she was really two years older than her profile stated. She told him this after they had shared a good introductory phone conversation and he had asked to meet her in person.

There was a long silence on his end of the phone.

"If I had known that was your age, I would not have called you."

"What?" Lucy asked. "I am only two years older than it states and that makes a difference to you?"

"Yes."

"Shallow beyond words," I responded when she told me this pathetic story.

Keeping her optimism was not easy. Either she did not want to meet someone after their first phone conversation, or she was excited about meeting and then eventually bored. We worked hard in finding the right words to say at the right time. Through it all Lucy tried to keep her hopes alive.

My phone rang. It was Lucy.

"My computer has a virus. It has sent messages to everyone in my e-mail address book. I am getting messages back from every guy I went out with, dated and broke up with. They are telling me they are thrilled to hear from me."

With that she started listing past names that I had helped free her from years ago. We were laughing so hard we could not breathe. The hours of good-bye speeches were erased electronically in an instant.

Lucy and I talk by phone almost every day. I have not heard from her in three days and will call her soon. I have a feeling she is on-line conversing with her past. I will have my work cut out for me.

CARDBOARD PEOPLE

I drive the same route everyday on my way to work. I am constantly amazed at the number of buildings being torn down and the construction of new apartment buildings going up. No sooner is a for sale sign placed on a completed building than a sold out sign follows almost immediately. This could be anywhere in urban America.

One morning as I was observing these new town houses and apartment buildings, I passed under an expressway. What I saw was another type of construction of an American home. This was not built by a Chicago union. This one was built by one person.

The viaduct served as the sky. The roof of this new house was a large piece of cardboard. The walls were bags from Carson's, the Chicago department store icon that just closed its doors.

How fitting, I thought, that the individual inhabiting this makeshift home decorated it with the last remnants of an American retail giant. Up and down this street, newness co-existed with the forgotten.

The following weekend my husband and I were doing errands. I was driving and my husband Richard was enjoying a morning Starbucks. As we passed a pharmacy, I pulled in and told him that I had one quick thing to pick up and that he could wait in the car. He asked me to dispose of his empty cup.

Holding the cup, I was ready to throw it away in a garbage bin in front of Walgreens when a man approached me and put money in my cup. I was speechless. Incredulous, I looked at the cup and then looked at him. He misunderstood and assuming that nonverbally I was asking for more, he put his hand in his pocket, put more money in my cup and told me that was all the change he had. I started laughing and explained what I had intended to do with the cup. Then he laughed and I gave him back his money.

My husband thought I should have stayed there to make a little extra change. My mother wanted to know what I was wearing.

We are a society conditioned to fill the cups of the homeless or to remove our eye contact and make them invisible. We have become neighbors with cardboard homes decorated with our trash. How many times have I watched concert subscribers walk past the woman asking for help with her cup while standing at the Symphony garage entrance? They look right past her as though she was not there. And what about the gentle fellow in a wheelchair who positions himself in front of a bustling Dairy Queen so that he can open the door for customers hoping for a tip in response? Walking in and out ignoring his presence and efforts, people act as if the door was automated.

What is most frightening to me is that we are becoming complacent with these images. They are there and we are familiar with them. They are annoyances in our way as we navigate our afternoon chores or our evening walk.

Sometimes they turn on us such as the homeless woman who lit a fire to keep warm thereby killing residents in the building and the man who stabbed people he passed on the street because he said they looked at him strangely.

They are anonymous and we wish to keep them that way. We cannot pollute our realities with theirs. Their existence reminds us of the frailty of our own good luck. In our eyes they are made only of cardboard cups and walls.

Seven

The Dream

MY BEST AUDIENCE

When I received the call from the President of Hadassah Chai Chapter inviting me to perform my stories, I was delighted. I had performed for other Jewish organizations but had not had the honor of performing for Hadassah.

From the moment I arrived at the meeting, I felt a warmth from the ladies that can only be described as a feeling of being home among one's own Jewish sisters. I mingled and enjoyed the high tea served with finger sandwiches, delicate sweets and lovely serving pieces.

When I was introduced to read my stories, I walked up to the lectern and looked at my audience. It was a wonderful turnout of about seventy women and one man, my beloved husband who never missed any of my performances.

My mother, sister Linda, dear friend Sandy and some special cousins were in attendance. But my guest of honor was my girlfriend Arlene who had flown in from Florida to Chicago to see my program. Every time I looked at my audience while performing a story, I would see my beloved childhood friend's face smiling at me.

I remember that afternoon for many reasons. As audience members, the Hadassah ladies and I fit like a hand and glove. They were with me through every emotion my words conveyed. As an author performing her own stories, nothing could be more thrilling than to feel the audience moving with you in sync.

My Hadassah audience was generous, supportive, responsive and filled with Jewish connection. The experience for me was unforgettable. Looking at the faces of the ladies I had just met sitting among my family and dearest friends was an exquisite feeling of gratitude.

After my program, my family and Arlene and I browsed some of the charming gift shops in a near-by suburb. In one of the shops, Arlene fell in love with a red friendship treasure box that I purchased for her as a surprise.

This box became a treasure to her. We referred to it often when speaking.

Recently, I went to see Arlene's daughter and her family who were in town for the weekend. Bari gave me back the box. I cried. When I opened the box, Arlene had saved many of my notes and quotes along with clippings she found about friendship that spoke of us.

I looked at this box and wondered why fate dictated that I now have it back. It was a confirmation that my friend had died several months before.

I have now put my notes from Arlene into the red friendship box with her notes from me and have placed the red box in a special place of honor in my home. When I look at the box, I feel I can touch my friend.

The Hadassah event was the last time I saw my friend. That afternoon was a blessing for me on so many levels. The Hadassah audience was among my best and most memorable.

MY GIFT OF NOW

At 11:00 a.m. every Thursday for the last thirteen years I have been in my college classroom teaching Communication with an emphasis on Public Speaking. For twenty years before that I was a college administrator and in television management. On this Thursday at 11:00 a.m. I am walking through the door of Chicago's Modern Art Museum. Why? Because I feel like it. I am free. I am retired. I am a tourist in my own city.

The Museum had a retro exhibit of Rock & Roll with a multimedia focus. As I danced from room to room, I suddenly stopped. The next display before me was a room with a floor constructed from and made up of vinyl records. These were the 33 LP's of my youth. I could not bring myself to walk into that room because walking on those records somehow seemed to me disrespectful. Visually the floor was an eye catcher. Literally, it represented my growing up years. At that moment I was a retiree in my new present looking at my childhood past.

A man standing across the way at the other entrance to the room looked up at me. Our eyes met and seemed to express a unified hesitation to walk on this floor made of records. Slowly as though symbolically holding hands we each entered the room. We stood on records to read the labels in front of us and behind us. We moved tentatively, two strangers with a shared grace of purpose and memory.

We nodded to one another as we left the floor of records. My day as a free woman had allowed me to revisit a time of youth that I will never forget. Yet I was acutely aware that I would not trade this present time in my life for any past reality. I was inspired by my new sense of freedom. I was exhilarated and could not wait to see what the rest of my day would bring me.

I left the museum. It was a sunny fall day in Chicago. I looked up at the sky. Its infiniteness reflected how I felt about my possibilities. This was chapter two of my life story and I was going to write, edit and publish it with an anticipation and energy I had never felt before.

I walked along Chicago's main shopping boulevard. As I passed the window of a luggage store, I saw it. There it was sitting on display. I stood staring at it. It was the most beautiful red leather briefcase I had ever seen.

I entered the store. I walked closer to the briefcase and stood looking at it. Then I picked it up and held it in my hands for the first time. The leather was smooth. There were ample pockets and compartments. The best part was that it was red. That color described the way I felt. Vibrant, excited, determined, on top of the world would just begin to express my state of mind.

I was now a published author. Writing was my third career, my chapter three. All that I needed was a briefcase to house my work. It could not be just any briefcase. It had to be the red one I was now swinging in my left hand as I walked around the shop.

I placed the briefcase on the counter and looked at the price tag. My heart sank. This was a bit more than I had hoped to spend. Suddenly a tag fell out of the case. It had '30% discount' written on it. I smiled. This was meant to be mine.

My husband had given me wise and insightful advice when I told him I planned to retire. He said that I should implement whatever I wanted to do before I retired so that I would hit the ground running. For me this advice was the reason my transition was a happy and less frightening one than it might have otherwise been. As a professional, I had worked my entire adult life. Whatever my next choices were, they had to be in place on the day I said good-bye to an educational and media career that I had cherished.

I had prepared myself well. I had my nonfiction stories coming out in an anthology and four magazines the three months following my retirement. This shiny red leather briefcase was my retirement gift to myself.

When I came home with my package, I gently unwrapped the case and placed it on my desk next to the clock I had been given for retirement and the engraved rocking chair I had been given when I was named the College's Distinguished Professor. A rocking chair, a clock and a red briefcase, what an interesting collection of symbols, I thought.

Like the 33 LP's, I would regard them as treasures of my past, present and future about which I would now write. Time is my gift of now.

ACKNOWLEDGMENTS

Edited versions of the stories in this collection were originally published in the following anthologies:

More Than Life	*Pushcart Prize Nominee* Thin Threads Moms & Grandmas (Kiwi Publishing, 2011) Forever Families (Mandinam Press, 2012)
The Red Pen	Forever Friends (Mandinam Press, 2008) Chicken Soup for the Soul: Grieving and Recovery (Chicken Soup for the Soul Publishing, 2011)
Her First Grandchild	Grandmother, Mother and Me (Hidden Brook Press, 2012)
Golden Hands	Grandfather, Father and Me (Hidden Brook Press, 2013)
Four Sisters in Life and Death	This I Believe On Love (John Wiley & Sons, Inc., 2011)
Twice in One Family	Forever Families (Mandinam Press, 2012)

The Revolving Door	Chicken Soup for the Chocolate Lover's Soul (Health Communications, Inc., 2007) Not Your Mother's Book On Being a Woman (Publishing Syndicate, 2012)
Please Be Anonymous	Too Much: Tales of Excess (Unknown Press, 2014)
The Ring	Forever Families (Mandinam Press, 2012)
The Needle in the Haystack	Contemporary American Women: Our Defining Passages (All Things That Matter Press, 2009)
Ronald	Chicken Soup for the Soul: True Love (Chicken Soup for the Soul Publishing, 2009)
Honey, Believe Me	Forever Travels (Mandinam Press, 2010)
The Hotel Balcony	Forever Travels (Mandinam Press, 2010)
The Room with No Room	Forever Travels (Mandinam Press, 2010)
Slippery and Waterless in Madrid	Forever Travels (Mandinam Press, 2010)
Unexpected	Forever Travels (Mandinam Press, 2010)
First in Line	Forever Travels (Mandinam Press, 2010) Chicken Soup for the Soul: Married Life! (Chicken Soup for the Soul Publishing, 2012)

The Holiday Diary	Forever Travels (Mandinam Press, 2010) Chicken Soup for the Soul: Christmas in Canada (Chicken Soup for the Soul Publishing, 2014)
A Tale of Two Vardas	Forever Travels (Mandinam Press, 2010)
RG	Joy, Interrupted (Fat Daddy's Farm Press, 2013)
Breakfast at Tiffany's... Almost	Forever Travels (Mandinam Press, 2010) Not Your Mother's Book On Travel (Publishing Syndicate, 2013)
Dancer's Lane	Press Pause Moments: Life Transitions by Women Writers (Kiwi Publishing, 2010)
Would You Like to Dance?	Fundamentally Female (Kittleson Creek Press, 2012, 2013)
Retracing Old Steps	Forever Families (Mandinam Press, 2012)
His Home	Forever Families (Mandinam Press, 2012)
Mr. X & Mr. Y	Forever Friends (Mandinam Press, 2008) Miracles & Extraordinary Blessings (Whispering Angel Books, 2014)
Dream Girl	Nurturing Paws (Whispering Angel Books, 2011) The Animal Anthology Project: True Tails (Xlibris, 2012) Not Your Mother's Book On Dogs (Publishing Syndicate, 2012)

The Elevator	Forever Friends (Mandinam Press, 2008)
The Hat	The Ultimate Teacher (Health Communications, Inc., 2009) Thin Threads Teachers & Mentors (Kiwi Publishing, 2010) Thin Threads Life Changing Moments (Kiwi Publishing, 2010) Living Lessons (Whispering Angel Books, 2010) Chicken Soup for the Soul: From Lemons to Lemonade (Chicken Soup for the Soul Publishing, 2013)
My Office	Press Pause Moments: Life Transitions by Women Writers (Kiwi Publishing, 2010)
There Forever	Miracles & Extraordinary Blessings (Whispering Angel Books, 2014)
Waiting	Thin Threads: Women & Friendship (Kiwi Publishing, 2011)
Life 101	Forever Friends (Mandinam Press, 2008)
My Best Audience	Thin Threads Hadassah Life Changing Moments (Kiwi Publishing, 2012)
My Gift of Now	Contemporary American Women: Our Defining Passages (All Things That Matter Press, 2009)

BIO

Elynne Chaplik-Aleskow is a Pushcart Prize-nominated author and award-winning educator and broadcaster. She is Founding General Manager of WYCC-TV/PBS and Distinguished Professor Emeritus of Wright College in Chicago. Her adult storyteller program *IN HER OWN VOICE* is renowned. Her stories and essays have been published in over 30 anthologies including Grandfather, Father & Me (Hidden Brook Press); Chicken Soup for the Soul Books (Simon & Schuster Distributor); This I Believe: On Love (Wiley Publishing); Forever Travels (Mandinam Press); Press Pause Moments (Kiwi Publishing); My Dad Is My Hero (Adams Media); Nurturing Paws (Whispering Angel Books) and various magazines including the international Jerusalem Post.

Elynne Chaplik-Aleskow's performances and discussions of her stories have been broadcast on The Bob Edwards Show on NPR, Rick Kogan's Sunday Papers on WGN radio, WBBM Newsradio with Regine Schlesinger, Conversations LIVE with Cyrus Webb and YouTube. Her three careers have been spotlighted on WCIU-TV's 26 North Halsted. She performed her Pushcart Prize-nominated memoir "More Than Life" in NYC at the Museum of Motherhood. Elynne has performed her stories for organizations throughout Chicago including the Printer's Row Lit Fest. Her work has been part of the production "Dear Mother" in L.A. at The Lyric Theater. Elynne was a featured guest artist performing her stories at the Acorn Theater in Michigan and at Chapters Bookstore in Ontario, Canada. A film short adaptation of Elynne's story "The Hat" was featured at a Chicago Indie film festival. Visit **http://LookAroundMe.blogspot.com**

Elynne's husband Richard is her muse.